GUN DOG

Revolutionary
Rapid
Training
Method

GUN
DOG

by

RICHARD A.
WOLTERS

Foreword by
John W. Randolph
Outdoor Editor NEW YORK TIMES

Pictures by
Joan Sydlow

A DUTTON BOOK

DUTTON
Published by the Penguin Group
Penguin Books USA Inc., 375 Hudson Street,
New York, New York 10014, U.S.A.
Penguin Books Ltd, 27 Wrights Lane,
London W8 5TZ, England
Penguin Books Australia Ltd, Ringwood,
Victoria, Australia
Penguin Books Canada Ltd, 2801 John Street,
Markham, Ontario, Canada L3R 1B4
Penguin Books (N.Z.) Ltd, 182–190 Wairau Road,
Auckland 10, New Zealand

Penguin Books Ltd, Registered Offices:
Harmondsworth, Middlesex, England

First published by Dutton, an imprint of New American Library, a
division of Penguin Books USA Inc. Distributed in Canada by
McClelland & Stewart Inc.

46 45 44 43 42 41 40 39

 REGISTERED TRADEMARK—MARCA REGISTRADA

LIBRARY OF CONGRESS CATALOGING CARD NUMBER:
61–9226

ISBN: 0-525-24549-9
Printed in the United States of America
Designed by Richard A. Wolters

Dedicated to dogs in the field.

Contents

Introduction

There is going to be a sharp public debate between Wolters and the old-line dog trainers, especially those whose dogma is that a dog cannot be trained before he is a year old. But that doesn't make any difference: there never has been much agreement between any two men or women who ever trained a dog or talked about training a dog.

The thing is that Wolters has some new stuff, developed by scientists fooling around with dogs as subjects in studies aimed at other ends, and new stuff always goes down hard, as when a Williams College undergraduate tries to swallow a cue ball on a bet.

A vital bit of new stuff is using the bird-wing as a training tool instead of a plaything to keep the dog amused and eager. I was present and taking pictures, all of which I blew for one reason or another, when Wolters taught his dog Beau to retrieve from the water at Pleasant Lake, N.H., by the use of the bird-wing. It took about ten minutes and was about the most impressive thing I ever saw, except for the time Lawton Carver stepped off a ledge and floated his hat while teaching some boys how to wade a trout stream safely.

I saw a good deal of Beau's training, in all of which the bird-wing played a prominent part, and got pretty sick of it. A dog ought to make a mistake once in a while, or get sulky or bat-headed, and it puts an uneasiness into the immortal soul of man when the brute starts to get infallible or even too consistent. I get to thinking that if somebody had trained me with a bird-wing I might not have flunked algebra, and that is not healthy thinking.

What is the use of talking about these pictures? They speak for themselves, and for Joan Sydlow, a pro, who took most of them. They even speak for Wolters and for a formidable histrionic gift.

It ought to be enough to say that this is the first time I have seen a dog-training book in which pictures fully and accurately illustrate every step of the training; every step in its order, with the trainer persuading or forcing the dog to do what is desired. These pictures, more than 200 of them, do this brilliantly.

But, because of careful planning and expert photography (the picture magazines always call it perceptive photography and I am sick of that, too), some of these pictures are much more. They are good to look at. Strained interpretation can never add anything to that.

Again, this book has stuff that some of the old-liners won't like because it is new and therefore different from what they have been doing for years. But it worked for Wolters and I think it will work for anybody who gives it a fair, intelligent trial. It is simple, rational, and orderly; and it does not pretend to be a field-trial formula.

Yet I think that if Wolters had taken a standard training procedure, and photographed it and written it and laid it out this way, it would still have been a sensational book — the first one, so far as I know, in which the reader can *see* everything that he has to do in schooling his own dog. It would have been quite a thing, too, if he had simply written the new stuff in the old way. This combination is matchless, like Wolters' sports coats and English cloth hats.

JOHN W. RANDOLPH
The New York Times

Author's Note

After one completes the work of writing a book, making the layouts for all the picture pages, styling and counting type until numbers start to float into one's dreams, the real pleasure comes — writing the acknowledgments.

It is hard to decide whom to acknowledge first — Beau, my English Setter, or Joan Sydlow who made the collection of fine dog pictures for this book. They both worked hard, but Beau, being a well trained male, I am sure, would defer to a lady.

Joan took over 2500 pictures for this book, and a finer collection of dog pictures would be hard to find. It only takes 1/200 of a second to take a picture. Multiply that by 2500 and it comes to about 12½ seconds of work. Actually it took months (to get these pictures), but Joan is used to this sort of thing. She has become one of the country's outstanding magazine photographers. I am only sorry that we cannot show more of her pictures here.

A most important acknowledgment must go to Dr. J. Paul Scott and his team of workers at the Animal Behavior Laboratory at Hamilton Station, of the Roscoe B. Jackson Memorial Laboratory, Mount Desert Island, Maine. When I first read the technical papers produced by Dr. Scott and his co-workers, giving all the new information about the mental development of a dog, my mind whirled with excitement and my eye couldn't get the material off the page fast enough. Many hunters, myself included, have been training puppies for the field at a very young age. Some have done it because they thought it was good practice, some because they were impatient. But, because this runs counter to general practice, we all rationalized our reasons one way or the other. Now, what was a by-gum-and-by-gumption training method has definite scientific proof.

I wish to thank Dr. Scott, Dr. Stanley, and Dr. Fuller for making my visit to their laboratory at Desert Island, Maine, a most productive one. I found the experiments they are conducting, basically for social psychology, most interesting. Their work on dogs is to help man understand himself better. As a by-product of this research, man can understand dog better, and dog can understand man better. Dr. Scott's work has given me the scientific proof needed to document this book.

My wife Olive, a graduate student at Columbia in Social Psychology, must receive credit for explaining to me some of the scientific gobbledygook that a poor layman must put up with when he enters the world of a specialized science.

My thanks must go to Yonda Reid of Harrison, Maine, who encouraged me to start the book and who was my strongest literary critic.

Gene Hill of the Jockey Hollow Field Trial Club is due credit for keeping me up late nights, drinking my whiskey, and arguing point by point all of my dog facts.

Henry P. Davis, author of *Training Your Own Bird Dog,* also fits into this picture. Although I haven't seen Henry in a dog's life, his personal tips when I started training will always be remembered.

A special mention to the members of the Midtown Turf, Yachting and Polo Association* who settle all kinds of hunting and fishing problems at the weekly luncheon at Manny Wolf's Chophouse on Third Avenue. As a member of this austere, aimless group who have discussed every phase of hunting with dogs, and have hunted every corner on the eastern coast (near a good tavern) I have this short statement to make — it's only about 30,000 words and something over 200 pictures . . . *read on.*

R. A. W.

---

* Hunting and fishing only.

Part I

Chapter 1

Why This Book

From his prehistoric beginnings man has possessed two things: woman and dog. This book is not going to teach man anything new about women, who are no longer possessions. It's going to deal strictly with dogs. Some of my friends have called me coward for this. I just don't figure it that way. If a man is going to sit down and write a book, he might as well write it about something he thinks he understands. With all this clear in my mind — I think — I've set out to write about man's best and oldest friend, the one that's still a possession.

Just as there are all breeds of women, there are all breeds of dogs, and one man couldn't sit down and write about them all, especially if it were to be a book on training.

This is a *gun dog* book for the upland bird hunter. A how-to-train book. I might as well, here now, tell you what we're *not* going to cover. We won't tell you how to housebreak your puppy, or how to feed him. You'll have to go elsewhere to find out how to build a kennel. Dog care, like combing, bathing, and so on, will be left to your own judgment. Your dog's health is up to your veterinarian. Let him teach you how to play doctor, if you must. You won't find a chapter in this book on the equipment for training — the collar, leash, whistle, *et al*. I will assume you know what they are and what they look like. The book will not contain a list of the latest field trial winners and field trial information. We will not be dealing with the field trial dog at all. Gun Dogs, that's it.

This dog is to be your hunting assistant and companion for upland game birds. The information will serve you whether it be a flushing dog or a pointing dog. Of course, the trainer with the flushing dog will have to skip the information on pointing.

Choosing the breed of dog is a decision that will be left up to you. Where you live has a lot to do with this. In a very hot climate you shouldn't run a long-haired dog, and the opposite is true in cold country. In certain areas one type of dog is more popular than others. If you're going to be a one-dog man and hunt with others in the same boat, it'll pay for all to have the same breed. You can have a lot of fun developing your own line of dogs. But, even more important, if your neighbor has a pointing dog and you get a flushing dog, he'll see to it that you both hunt — separately.

Why a new book on dog training?

Don't think for one moment that this book is just a rehash of the same material that good men have written on this subject in the last fifty years. If that's all I thought I was going to do in this book, I would've better spent my time researching a good fast novel on women, or a good novel on fast women.

GUN DOG *is a revolutionary rapid training method. It's new. It's never been presented before, and we will explain new scientific findings about the learning habits of dogs that will startle the old-time trainers.*

A revolutionary rapid training method is needed. For better or for worse, the 1950's brought a tremendous change in our hunting picture in America. Since the last war, a social revolution has taken place. After taxes, Americans seem to be able to eke out enough money to spend a rather tidy sum on their new-found leisure time. This has put a lot of new hunters in the field. What used to be a handful of bird hunters has literally multiplied into millions. The open land, teeming with game, has shrunk behind posted signs or has been turned into your housing development. Plenty of land and an abundance of game were always necessary ingredients for dog training. We had all of this — but no more. Less land — less game — more hunters — these have complicated the dog training picture for today's hunter in the moderate income bracket.

But, in spite of the new odds against him, once a man's been smitten with the smell of powder and excited by the flush, he's hooked. He might as well start right away to skimp on lunch and save for that fine double-barrel.

The new gun, the new world of the outdoors — its smells, its beauty, its companionship, its relaxation — will carry him through the first season or so. But, upland game shooting is a sport with a long history and centuries of tradition in which the dog plays a major role. Inevitably, the hunter stumbles across the great literature that's been passed down to us. Devoted and intelligent men have given him a drama based on rich and satisfying experiences of hunter and hunting dog. For generations they have co-starred. The script was written in the sixteenth century, and the lines have never changed. When the curtain falls on *Man and Dog*, their loyalty, companionship, devotion leave the audience in silence.

It's not only tradition that impels the hunter to own a trained hunting partner. He comes to realize through experience that in these days of scarce game he's more than likely to go home with an empty bag if he doesn't have a dog.

Although it's true, that the lines of the play have not changed, we can see of late that the set has been altered completely. How can a man living on a hundred and fifty feet of land, or in an apartment, own and train a hunting dog? I can hear them now, "I would love to own a good pointing dog, but. . . ." His desire is not based solely on the need — man has an affinity for a fine working dog. He wants a trained dog for all the reasons given, and more, but hesitates. He's afraid, merely because he hasn't been shown how to do it in a way that will work, within the framework of present-day conditions. This is today's dilemma.

How many times have you heard the little woman say: "Having a dog around is like having another child in the house." If she says it in a defiant tone, this book won't help you with that problem, unless you strike her with it. If there's a certain amount of affection in her voice, you have the go-ahead signal, and an important training clue, a dog is like a child.

Because of a changing world we are not training our kids in school today the same way you were trained when you were a boy. Or maybe it's because we've learned a lot of new things about the way kids learn. We've all kinds of teaching devices now that we never had in the one-room schoolhouse. Take a look at the school tax you paid last year. Things have changed. Hunting conditions have changed too. So, it's time that we took a new look at our dog training methods. This book is that new look.

The material in this book is directed to the man who will have one dog, and that dog will double as the family pet, and not the family pest. You're living in an apartment or a home in the suburbs; the only game you will have nearby is poker. If, on the other hand, you have five dogs and land with game on it, this book will help speed up your training too.

We're going to tell you the right age of the pup, *in days*, when he should be started in his training. You, as a one-dog hunter, can't sit around waiting for this puppy to grow up before you can hunt with him. We are going to show you how to train the puppy so that he will be hunting with style when he's six months old, and most puppies will be ready before that. You're going to be able to take this puppy into the field with your cronies, with no embarrassment, and he'll do a damn fine job.

We're going to take new advantage of training tools. The most important one will be a fishing rod with a bird wing attached to the line. The student architect doesn't learn his job by constructing buildings; it would take him too long to learn his whole profession, and it would be too expensive. With today's hunting conditions, same with training a dog. Training tools are going to save you a lot of time and money, but one of the most important reasons for using the teaching aids is to give the dog an incentive for all he has to learn. Since hunting in the field is not as accessible as it once was, more of our training will take place in the yard.

What's to be required of you? Common intelligence applied every day and a will to stick to the job. If you're just going to fool around, do it at a bar. If you're a traveling salesman, it's better that you read and learn from books on women. You'll have more contact with them than with dogs. A dog's not going to require too much of your time, but you're going to have to be home to teach school.

What speed do you take your dog at? Whatever speed he takes you at. Don't be afraid to push him. I show you the indicators to watch for, let them guide you.

For goodness' sake, stop worrying whether you can do it. One fellow with seven kids at home told me he'd hate to try to train a dog — "Don't think I'd know how." He was willing to take a chance on seven kids, but for some reason he feels a dog would lick him. We all like to think there's great reward in teaching children, but don't underestimate a dog. While you're training him you'll do a lot of thinking. No matter what system a man uses in training a dog, a dog will teach a man more about himself than he ever knew before.

Man has written flowery prose and has said much about the wonders of the hunting dog and himself. Some of it *might* be true.

Chapter 2

The Economic Factors of a Dog

When you've brought the dog home from the kennel and you've given him some food and a little milk, that's the first payment in advance. As he starts to sniff around the "new big kennel," gives all members of the family a few kisses then falls asleep in a corner, he's accepted the job. The two of you have just signed a business contract. The pup doesn't know yet who the boss is — that's *you*. And — the boss should have some definite ideas about the assets of his new business partner.

Ninety-five per cent of the 26 million dogs in this country are flea bags and affectionate parasites. For nothing more than a little companionship, a wag of the tail, they get room and board, medical care, social security, plush living, unemployment compensation, plus your easy chair. What kind of a business deal is that?

Your puppy is to be the worker — you the boss. Let's get that straight from the start. Eventually, if he does his job well, he'll be made a full-fledged partner.

If not, *get rid of him*. Now, I'm serious about this. I've seen more guys waste money and, what's more important still, *time,* on problem dogs.

As an example, a professional trainer told me about an exceptionally handsome dog that was given to him because the dog wouldn't hunt. He brought the dog around, but it took months. Every day he walked the dog on a very short leash while he trained the other dogs on birds. At first the dog paid no attention. Soon he showed interest in what the other dogs were doing. Finally he almost went beside himself to get out and get one of those birds. "How many flushes did it take?" "Oh, a couple hundred," answered the trainer.

You most likely won't see that number of birds in two seasons. As a weekend hunter you can't possibly cope with that kind of dog problem. *Get rid of such a dog!*

Now, what about your investment. You paid good money for the fool. Forget it. It'll cost you more in hard-earned cash to feed such a dog for one year than the original investment. He'll eat just as much as a producing dog — one who pays dividends.

I'm assuming that you live, more or less, as I do. I haven't seen a pheasant or a grouse near my little suburban plot of land in the fourteen years that I've been living there. Neither have any of my dogs, to the best of my knowledge. Major corrective measures are something that we, as weekend hunters, can't fool with. We have jobs to go to every day. We have *all* the mouths in the family to feed — not just the new one.

What are you going to pay for your future partner? If he's good it won't make any difference if you pay thirty-five dollars or a hundred and fifty dollars. I've paid both of these prices and have had great dogs. A lot has to do with circumstances. I emphasize here that in both cases I, or good friends, hunted over the parents of the pups. This, at least, gave me some indication of what I was getting.

In the case of the thirty-five-dollar dog the owner had two litters at once. He had pups coming out of the furniture. The price was low. He wanted someone else to have the headaches — but fast. I know — I've sold pups. The first ones that went brought a hundred dollars, then the pressure got so great around the house that the last one was practically given away. The hundred-and-fifty-dollar puppy was bought from one of the finest kennels in the country. I spent a day hunting over the bitch; I spoke to a hunter that shot over the sire. I was satisfied. With tears rolling down my cheeks I parted with the money.

Seriously speaking, I firmly believe that the original cost is minor as compared with the vet bills, food, and so on — to say nothing of the cost of weekend hunting trips which stand to be ruined if you buy a stubborn, headstrong mule instead of a hunting dog.

But, beware of a bargain dog. If you can't hunt over the parents or talk to someone who has, you may pay little — and get little. Don't be fooled by pedigree papers. Tell the slick salesman who keeps running his fat fingers over the fifth generation of ancestors, and babbling fancy names, that you're interested in the parents and grandparents. The parents each produce 50 per cent of your dog; the grandparents 25 per cent each. The fifth generation which may boast of aristocratic lineage contributes only 6¼ per cent of your dog, and that 6¼ per cent of your dog might not be the part that hunts.

Remember, this is a business deal. Deal with legitimate people. Get a line on the kennel, and — hell's bells — make sure you're dealing in *hunting* stock, not show queens. Show dogs have been bred to live on the fat of the land. The only feathers they've ever seen were on the hat of some female judge.

As boss this is going to cost you, so you might as well go to the right employment agency. The *Field Dog Stud Book* run by the *American Field* in Chicago, is the authority for field dogs.

You can teach a dog *how* to hunt but you can't teach him *to* hunt. So you should be sure of his immediate hunting background. As boss, when you hire someone in your office you check on his references. When you show the new employee where the water cooler is, his background indicates that he's not going to stand there all day. But, if his references prove wrong you get rid of the water-logged deadwood. A working partner in the field is no different from one in the office. When a guy starts on a new job he's on trial, whether he knows it or not.

I always prepare my family ahead of time when a new dog is coming into our home. First, we have an understanding: This dog has a job. By the time I know whether or not he's the dog for the job, we'll all have fallen in love with him. But if he doesn't work out, we also all know that Daddy will find a good home for him, where he can eat the pocket out of some other guy's pants. I just don't have room for him. Besides, we have all kinds of pets. Mother has a poodle that sits in my chair; son has a fish in a leaking tank; daughter has a bird that won't sing, and I know there's a turtle somewhere around. Thank goodness I've never had to find a home for a dog, but I'm prepared to if he's useless.

Perhaps the economics of a dog sound more like a wake than the joy of a birth. It's not always so. I remember a time a few years ago, when I made arrangements to get a dog from upstate. I knew the parents, hunted with the owner, and arranged to have the dog delivered at seven weeks of age. The big day came and I took the afternoon off from work — he was to arrive at 3 P. M. I suggested that my wife take a grouse out of the freezer to celebrate the occasion for, I reasoned, it was fitting that we "taste game" in honor of the new arrival. One grouse would be plenty. I was too excited to eat, my son was not going to be home, and baby daughter never eats. Then the trouble started. Grandmother and Grandfather came over to see the new puppy and my son came home, after all, to see the new puppy and my friend arrived exactly at suppertime with the new puppy. I counted the noses — seven! I counted the grouse — one! Yes, it was fitting and proper that we "taste game" in honor of the occasion — and taste it is all we did.

Chapter 3

Critical Periods of a Dog's Learning

Starting a puppy and how a dog learns go hand in hand. Any animal that is going to be trained should receive the training as soon as it is ready to accept it. This prevents the learning of bad habits and the difficult process of unlearning. The time to start a puppy will then depend on his *mental* development. Sending a puppy to school in the past was based solely on the physical development of the dog. Unfortunately for many dogs and trainers the boat was missed. This was not the fault of the trainer. He didn't have information available on the mental growth of a puppy. Since he didn't have the facts, old wives' tales became the basis for much gratuitous advice. But now, hand-me-down philosophies of dog training are as the sulfer-and-molasses cure for pneumonia.

I know a hunter who trains his dog strictly according to misconceptions. One of his favorites is the comparison between a dog's age and a man's age. The age ratio is one to seven. His reasoning starts this way. A seven-year-old dog corresponds to a forty-nine-year-old man, both past their prime. So far it sounds true enough. Then, he continues, training a three-months-old puppy is like sending a two-year-old to the first grade. When this hunting friend saw a six-month-old puppy hunting under fine control he attributed it to another old wives' tale — luck. But when the owner pointed out, "Luck, hell! I've worked with this dog for months," he answered, "You took a chance, could have ruined the dog." We now know the seven-to-one ratio is a physical ratio, not a mental one.

The hunter who started his training very early was doing it by instinct. But his instinct was right. Now we have the facts.

But, let's start at the beginning and see if we can unravel some of these old ideas. When do we start the puppy?

Let's set up an experiment. Put a child in a fenced-in area when he is old enough to be weaned. Provide shelter, a bed, feed him, get a doctor when necessary, make the pen big enough so that he can run and get exercise. Then when he is seven years old turn him loose to go to school. Can you imagine teaching manners, let alone a profession to such an animal? Yet, *this is what we have been told to do with our dogs.* When you think about it, common sense should tell us that there is something wrong. Old wives reveled in problem tales, but it takes knowledge to find a solution. Pavlov's experiments with dogs told us much about the behavior of man. Let's reverse it — see what the experiments on man can teach us about the behavior of dogs.

In Germany, problems of isolated children were studied for the first time with foundling children. The purpose of the experiment was to discover what language the children would speak if they had no exposure to the spoken word. The infants had no contact, except for the absolute necessities of life. The experiment was never completed. Without human contact and love the children died.

This led to a study of infants in a foundling home that was understaffed to such a degree that, although they had some contact with language and adults, they were left largely to their own devices. When these children were later placed in normal home situations, it was found that their capacity for learning was impaired. They were unable to form normal relationships with people, and this interfered with their ability to learn.

I've seen this happen many times with dogs. The answer seems obvious. If a puppy lives in a kennel too long with no human contact and training, when you buy him and take him home, you're adding a great big unknown factor to your training problem. Dog people have a term for it, "He's a good pup, well-bred, but a little sensitive." Sensitive, hell! The dog's just insecure. As a weekend trainer you're going to have to use much preventive medicine in your training. Serious problems have to be avoided.

It is only logical that the pup should come to you with no problems, and that you should have control over his development from the beginning. Other trainers vary in their thinking according to which of these old wives' tales fits their experience best as to when to start a dog. Some books say six months, some say a year, some go as far as to a year and a half. The most cautious, who don't want to be pinned down, say it depends on the dog. They are all wrong. New scientific findings leave no doubt about it. When do we take a puppy home? When do we start him? *Buy your puppy and take him home at the exact age of forty-nine days!* This is not an old wives' tale. It is based on scientific fact.

Dr. J. Paul Scott, social psychologist, Rhodes scholar, and director of the Animal Behavior Laboratory at Hamilton Station of the Roscoe B. Jackson Memorial Laboratory, Mount Desert Island, Maine, directed a project to help Guide Dogs for the Blind, Inc., in their dog training program.

An important finding was made: There are five critical periods of a pup's life. They all take place before the dog is sixteen weeks old.

FIRST CRITICAL PERIOD — 0 TO TWENTY-ONE DAYS

The research showed that *all* puppies of all breeds have mental capacities of almost zero until they are twenty-one days old. For these first three weeks the pup's needs are food, warmth, sleep, and his mother. Abruptly on the twenty-first day, the puppy's brain starts to function. It has been likened to an electric circuit that is of no value until the current has been applied. Until that point, the puppy's only drive is for survival.

SECOND CRITICAL PERIOD — TWENTY-ONE TO TWENTY-EIGHT DAYS

During his fourth week the puppy has an absolute need for Mama. His senses are functioning and all of a sudden the big new world has opened up all around him. His brain and nervous system start to develop. At no other time in his life will the emotional and social stresses of life have as great an impact. Removal from Mother at this time is drastic.

THIRD CRITICAL PERIOD — TWENTY-EIGHT TO FORTY-NINE DAYS

For the next three weeks the puppy will venture from its mother and examine the world around him. At the end of this period his nervous system and brain will have developed to the capacity of an adult, but of course without the experience. He will learn to recognize people and respond to voices. The pecking, or social order, of the litter starts to form. A little competition in his family life is a good thing, too much is harmful. The puppy is ready to learn during this third period. Before too much of his personality is formed, he should be weaned and taken from his litter mates and mother.

FOURTH CRITICAL PERIOD — FORTY-NINE TO EIGHTY-FOUR DAYS

When you take your puppy home at seven weeks, he will be physically immature, but his brain will have attained full adult form.

Dr. Scott's research has proved that this is the best time in a dog's life to establish dog-human relationships. This is why you, the trainer, should be in the picture at this most important time. The person who feeds him will take the place of his mother. The attachments the puppy makes now will permanently affect his attitude toward accepting direction and education. Let me repeat this, it's important to you as a trainer. Seven to twelve weeks is the time most conducive to beginning training and establishing a permanent relationship with his boss, you — the trainer. The dog started to learn in the third period. And during this, the fourth critical period, considerable teaching can be done. Simple commands can be taught in the form of games. There need be no discipline, but he can be shown how to

SIT, STAY, COME, HEEL, and even be started on a leash. Even getting settled in his new house at seven weeks is part of his education. How to handle the puppy during this period will be covered in the "Preschool" chapter. p. 26

A puppy, like a child, is going to learn, no matter what his situation. During the tender years we wouldn't dream of allowing our children to be taught by just anyone. And certainly we keep our offspring out of situations where they're likely to pick up bad habits from other kids. The puppy's like the kid.

For example: The puppy should not be left in the litter during this fourth period. In that environment he may become either a headstrong bully or a wallflower, depending upon where he falls in the family social structure. And, if left to his own devices at this age, he is likely to get "kennel blindness." He's going to learn, but from his kennel mates — and from occasional human contacts — attitudes contrary to what you will want.

It doesn't matter *what* the child or puppy learns in kindergarten, provided that it is good experience. If they like school, and they like the teacher, the stage is set. They will enjoy learning, and they will learn to learn.

To sum up this most important critical period: Establishing rapport with a puppy at this age will have a permanent good effect on his accepting directions and later education. The foundation of the training will be more or less in the form of games, just like the kids in kindergarten. This is the time to bind the dog to human control.

FIFTH CRITICAL PERIOD — EIGHTY-FOUR TO ONE HUNDRED TWELVE DAYS

This is the last critical stage in the puppy's educational development. The period between twelve and sixteen weeks is the time the young dog will declare his independence. Man and dog resolve who is to be boss. The social and educational preconditioning that went on in the fourth period helps the dog through this crucial time. The pup will try you for size, but the preventive medicine of the early lessons will make your job easier. Informal games stop — formal lessons start. This is the time the dog is ready to learn disciplined behavior. We will show how to handle this in the chapter, "The Puppy Goes to School."

A dog that has been cooped up with no human contact and training can be started in the early part of this fifth period, but he will never make up what he has lost earlier. He will never develop to his full potential. Just how lucky you will be is hard to say, but preschool training in the fourth period is your insurance against bad luck in this fifth period or the future.

13

Understanding these stages of the dog's mental growth will save the trainer time and headaches. Deciding who is boss could be settled later, but it might take a 2 × 4 to do it.

Dr. Scott's research has shown that a dog that has had *no* human contact before it is sixteen weeks old has little chance of becoming the sort of dog we would want as a companion. But, the most startling fact for the hunter who needs a trained dog, not just a companion is that the finest bred dog in the world may become completely untrainable, after the age of thirteen *weeks*, if he is left in the kennel just to exist and wait for an owner.

Take the battle out of the training job, get and start your dog at the right time — seven weeks — that's forty-nine days old.

Chapter 4
It's a Dog's Life — How He Learns It

"You can't teach an old dog new tricks." This ancient adage must have been written by some canny old dog living on Social Security. He had it pretty good — why change? But to be accurate, that venerable saying should be rewritten: "An old dog that has been taught nothing can learn nothing." A dog that has learned to learn, will be able to continue to learn as he grows older.

Just how does a dog learn? A lot depends on what is being taught and when. But, with a dog, you have one important factor in your favor. *He wants to please!* This is a valuable tool for you. Some forward-thinking cave man must have thrown some starving mutt a fat bone, and for the millions of years since man has had a grateful friend.

The dog responds to your display of pleasure or displeasure. There's always tension in the learning situation. Reward reduces this tension. Reprimand or punishment builds the tension. A dog's instinctive desire — to please — leads him to seek the reward of your good graces. He tries to do what you want. He is learning!

The stronger you can build this urge to please, the easier the training is going to be on both of you. Common sense on your part will show the way to properly balance rewards and punishments to get the learning mechanism started. At first it is all-important to instill and intensify this urge to please.

If your dog doesn't follow the usual pattern of wanting to please, I'll bet ninety-nine to one you didn't start him at the right age. But, in that one case, if he's not anxious to please, and he's not responding to his lessons, *get rid of him.*

Don't mistake a bold dog for a dog that does not want to please. A dog that doesn't want to please is either mean, too scared, too stupid, too lethargic, too wild, too nervous, or too timid. We'll show later in the "Preschool" chapter that by starting the training at the proper time we'll prevent these attitudes from cropping up. A bold pup is trainable. You'll have to use stronger measures to get him under control; you may have to advance slowly with a bold dog. The trainer must adjust his pace to the dog's personality and ability. He will find he can go faster with a smart and cooperative dog than with a slow or stubborn one. There is no exact training schedule. You will have to make your own.

Dogs are taught on both the conscious and unconscious levels of learning.

Learning on the unconscious level is learning a dog does without being aware that he is learning. This is done by the trainer putting the dog repeatedly in a controlled situation and having this situation repeated so many times that the dog reacts in a predictable manner as he learns to accept the situation as normal. You set up the problem, the dog must find the answer himself. Usually, in this unconscious training there is no punishment for lack of progress, no obvious reward given for achievement. Some examples of this are: preparation for the gun, learning to live in a car on hunting trips, the place of the dog in the field, and following directions by hand signal.

Learning on the conscious level is when a dog knows damn right well that he is being taught something. This is the formal lesson. Here is where the dog's desire to please is vital. Here's where common sense, love, affection, firmness and more firmness are the teacher's devices.

This learning process is all a matter of repetition, more repetition, and still more repetition until it becomes a part of the dog's behavior. Then we call it memory. This method may also be called learning by association.

You show the dog what you want. By trial and error he finds out what your language means. Once he has the idea, you put him through the action and give the command. He soon associates the command with what you expect of him. Then by repetition you cement this in his noggin.

Now, the good part about all this is that you as the trainer do not have to be smart. I've seen some rather sad humans train some good dogs. When you try to teach a kid geometry, you have to be able to do geometry, but you don't actually have to fetch to teach it to a dog, and what's more you'd look rather foolish doing it. All that is required is that you put the dog into the correct situation and give the command and then use some common sense. But that does not mean trying to reason with the dog. He can't understand your complicated gibberish.

I remember hunting in a party with a guy a few years ago whose dog wanted to hunt only with another party a half mile away. After incessant whistling and calling, the dog decided to come back. He lay down at his "trainer's" feet and panted — tongue down to his knees. The trainer, in a conversational tone, told the dog he should have come and obeyed the whistle. He then proceeded to tell him why. At this point I'd had enough.

I walked away. *So did the dog.* Soon the mutt got his breath and was off again to his new friends who were now going into the cover I had my eye on. The "trainer," with a sheepish look on his face, asked, "What can you do with a dog like that?" No one answered. But we sure thought. . . . A good thrashing would straighten that dog out, and if that didn't work, I'd give him to Aunt Minnie to protect her at the firemen's picnic.

There's just one more thing about a dog's learning. I disagree with most trainers who say that a dog should be taught one thing at a time. It's like a kid playing with building blocks, he builds one upon the other. When he knocks it over, he starts from the bottom and builds up higher and higher each time. He is not just learning how to put the top block on better, he's also learning to build a better base. It's the same with a pup. You build upon the things that are known, adding new things and broadening the meaning of things already learned. You start with one command, go on to the next and the next. In this way you also build a firm foundation for the basic commands, the teaching goes faster, and the pup gets a better idea of the whole picture. For example: When you teach a dog to COME, you would first give commands that he already knows — SIT, STAY — then teach COME. The foundation of the first two basic commands is made stronger by this repetition. But I can't see anything wrong with putting the dog on a leash as soon as this COME lesson is over and teaching him to HEEL while you two walk to the corner drugstore for some aspirin.

Chapter 5

How to Conduct the Lessons

Did you ever hear of the guy out West who acquired quite a reputation for training mules? His method was unique. He used soft, sweet talk — honey-coated words, gentle voice, and most of all, kindness. Hearing about this remarkable humane achievement, the Society for the Prevention of Cruelty to Animals decided to present this fine fellow with a medal. Someone's Aunt Minnie was chosen to do the honors and she arrived at the ranch, the award clutched to her bosom. Prior to the presentation ceremony she suggested a demonstration of these most exemplary training methods. The trainer obligingly trotted out one of his psychologically oriented mules, reached for a 2 × 4, and clobbered the beast over the think tank. As the mule staggered to his feet the lady emissary cried out in horror: "My good man, I thought you trained these mules with kindness!"

"Oh, I do, Ma'am," he answered quietly, "but first I have to get their attention!"

THE TEACHING ROLE

The stage has to be set for the lessons. The mule trainer used a 2 × 4 to do it. Some dog trainers ought to have a 2 × 4 used on them. They get fine dogs but lose sight of their own role as teacher before the pup is even out of grammar school. Reason? They fall too much in love with their dogs. That's the only objection to allowing a hunting dog to become a house pet. There's temptation to forget that this new child has a job to do. All breeds of upland bird dogs are very affectionate critters. But, beware — the dog will set a trap for you. A dog is just as smart at feeling you out in a training situation as you're supposed to be. He knows that you want him to show affection. He also learns that if he puts on a sad face, a hurt look, a put-upon pose, you may melt and stop the lesson. If you do, the dog's got you. Then you'll try to find an excuse: "Guess he's a sensitive pup, I'll have to go easy." This is a major error. But it's easy to recognize. If the dog shows that he's happy and normal in his everyday environment he's good material. But if he puts on the "hurt" act during training sessions, and you fall for it, *he's smarter than you are* and he'll train *you*. *Remember this:* he'll try you out just as you tried your teachers when you were in school.

During lessons, the teacher-pupil relationship must be rigidly maintained. Learning is never easy, but by using firmness sprinkled with affection, the dog will soon learn that he can't evade his lessons, and you're over a big hump. There's a wide difference between a dog lover and a dog trainer. The trainer accomplishes two things. He loves his dog, and also teaches his dog to work. The lover accomplishes only one thing. A dog can be ruined for hunting if he is loved but not trained.

Let's face it, saints have patience, hunters haven't. It's not patience a trainer needs, it's common sense. Dogs, like children, can be spoiled by too much patience. If a dog learns that he can get away with murder, he'll pick and choose which orders he will follow. Therefore, the first step in conducting lessons is to get into the role of teacher. Let's have no nonsense — let's get down to work!

THE REPRIMAND

Everybody knows how to love a dog. A pat, a caress, a kind word — they eat it up.

But the reprimand is more tricky. It may take many forms and vary in degree. I don't mean just in the degree of laying a leash across his back. You can hurt a dog just as much by completely ignoring him. For example, if you're trying to teach SIT and STAY, but he gets up and comes to you, *ignore him.* He comes to you expecting a pat, a kind word. Don't give him the time of day. This hurts his sense of pride. Just walk him back and start all over again. He'll know there's something not just right.

A dog instinctively recognizes a threatening gesture. If you're sure he understands what you want him to do, but suspect he's just testing you, come at him with an upraised hand. That'll soon make him fold. I usually take my hat off and use it as the threatening weapon. If the dog's just trying to assert his independence, this is not a thrashing offense. Here's where you have to use your judgment. Consider the degree of the offense. Take into account the circumstances, the age of the dog, and whether he should have known better — then mete out the punishment.

When he becomes downright ornery and stubborn there's only one way to straighten him out. Heaven protect me from Aunt Minnie and her every-third-Tuesday-meeting-of-the-ASPCA, but I'm going to say it. Thrash the dog. Do it with fervor, but with intelligence. I clip the dog with the folded leash until he cries out once. I talk angrily while I swing and continue to speak in a firm tone after the outcry to be sure it registered. Then

I switch over to a pleasant tone of voice and begin the lesson all over again. It's very important to get the situation back to normal as quickly as possible. Don't nag. This clean-cut discipline is not cruel as some think. It's kind. Any right-thinking parent will do it to his child. Failure to discipline is crueler.

Before you reprimand, be sure you have the facts straight. In yard training the facts are right before you, but when you transfer the training to the field it won't be quite so easy. Bob Zwirz, a hunting buddy, told this story last winter:

He had just taught Mindie, his setter, to fetch. She took to the training like a retriever. After a three-day rain, they went out to hunt. Mindie pointed a cock pheasant. Bob flushed it and took two shots. He thought the bird went down. The command FETCH was given.

Two hours later the dog still had not shown up. Bob was talking to himself by this time. "She'll never do this again. When that bitch comes home, I'll — I'll — she'll never do *this* again." Four hours later Mindie dropped the cock bird at Bob's feet.

It wasn't until about a week later that he found out what actually had happened. A neighbor came up to him on the street and said sympathetically: "Too bad about Mindie, she was such a good pup. I hated to see that pup drown." Bob was puzzled for a moment then, as the neighbor talked on he was able to piece the whole thing together. When the bird flushed he'd only winged it, and it had flown across the river. Mindie saw this, swam the river which was in flood condition from the three-day rain, and what the neighbor saw was Mindie on her way back with the bird in her mouth being swept downstream to her certain death.

One thought has plagued Bob ever since. *What if she'd had to drop the bird in order to save her own life?* When she got home he would have whaled the dickens out of her.

Beau, the dog in these pictures, had his life saved by a damn good, thrashing. He just pushed me too far when he was learning to SIT and STAY. He knew what I wanted but one night he decided that there were more important things to do — like ignoring me. I thrashed the hell out of him. The next night he was in the car with my wife when she came to meet the commuter train. When he saw me from across the street he got so excited he jumped out of the car window to run and greet me. A truck came flying down the street. I screamed the command: "SIT! STAY!" He froze. He was still sitting when the truck passed. One step more and he would have been killed. That spanking paid off.

NO TIPPING, PLEASE

A pat, a caress, or a little rough play along with some friendly talk should be the A's and B's on the dog's report card while in school. You will see in the field later that the excitement of the hunting itself will be his pay check for a job well done. He'll expect loving only when you all stop for a breather and a smoke. I do not believe in paying off a dog by shoving food into his mouth every time he does something that he was bred to do. I like to think that the training is taking place in the head, not the stomach. A kind word in his ear is making his brain work, food in the stomach only makes the bowels work. Besides, it's damn inconvenient to have a pocket full of tidbits. I hunted with a fellow who trained his dog on milk bone biscuits. We ran into some fast and furious woodcock shooting. His dog handled the first bird beautifully. The reward, for a job well done, was a milk bone. That was the last biscuit that dog had in the field. Another woodcock flushed, whistled, gave us a passing shot. In his excitement to reload, my partner shoved dog biscuits into his double. You should have heard what he said!

THE TONE OF VOICE

The tone of your voice is most important in training. The tone of command is as important as the command itself. Beginning trainers often beg their dogs to follow orders. There is just no place for baby talk in dog training. It's a command you are giving, not a request.

The tone quality of the voice can encourage the pup to go on and do what is expected. When a dog starts to putter around, a good rousing *"Hey, you! What's going on?"* will do the trick. If the dog is close by, the first command should be soft but firm. If you get no action, raise the voice. If you have to tell him the third time, let your neighbors hear it.

COMMANDS — SHORT AND BRISK

Commands should be short, brisk, single words: SIT, FETCH, WHOA, COME, NO, etc. Don't add a lot of gibberish to the commands. For example, don't say "SIT boy — come on, fellow — now come on — no, no, JACK — try it again, SIT!" This will get you nowhere. It is confusing to a dog. In that series of commands you were asking the dog to do one thing, but four commands were given — SIT, COME, NO, and JACK. The name should not be added to the command. The name is a separate command for attention.

Heavens to Betsy, give a hunting dog a short, snappy name like Jack, Mike, Jed, Queen, Fly, Belle! Leave the fancy ones on the pedigree. The name should not sound like another command. I made that mistake in calling the dog I am now working with Beau. I noted a little confusion on his part when I started to teach him WHOA. Beau and WHOA are too close in tone and sound quality.

I know a hunter who changed his dog's name. His first mistake was to let his young daughter name the pup. She named the setter Lovely Lady, and she was. The hunter trained the pup. On the first trip with his hunting cronies, the pup decided to investigate the world. Angered by his misbehavior the hunter took off, hell-bent-for-election, crashing through the woods, calling the dog at the top of his voice — LOVELY LADY — LOVELY LADY. . . .

YOUR STANCE AND MOVEMENTS

In conducting the lessons, how you look to the dog is important. Your body movements and position will influence the dog's response. Your movements should be slow and deliberate, never quick and jerky. Never rush at the pup to make a correction. Move in slowly and start the lesson all over.

Your body position can make the difference between just doing what he is told and doing it with enthusiasm. The two pictures show this. The upright stance does not appear to the dog to be as friendly a position. You command COME as in Picture 2, and he will obey — but, bend over, Picture 3, and he'll come-a-running. Since a dog can't really understand your language he uses all kinds of aids to understand you. Ever notice when you approach a strange dog, if you put your hand out from a standing position he will be cautious. If you bend over and meet him on his own level, he'll lick your face. Standing over a dog is a threat to him. In the early schooling period, bend over, show him you're a friend.

We have already mentioned that the dog learns many things on the unconscious level. The basic training of the commands is done with the voice. Hand signals and the whistle come into play as reinforcements for the voice. The stance you take while giving voice commands with hand signals is important. By repetition the dog associates the voice command with the supporting signal. With no effort on your part he will unconsciously learn the supporting signal as a substitute for the voice. Right from the beginning of the formal lessons the signals that reinforce the voice should be used. They will be explained in detail in the chapter, "The Pup Goes to School."

When you drive your car to town, the cop at the intersection raises his hand, palm out toward you: he reinforces the command by blowing his whistle, you stop. But either the upraised hand or the whistle alone would have you automatically reaching for your brake. I'm not suggesting that you have your dog drive you to town. I'm merely trying to show you that your dog learns to respond exactly the way you do — same mechanism.

2. Stand erect, call him. He'll come, but reluctantly. He feels this position is a threat. A dog quickly reads your attitude in your stance. Get him responding with enthusiasm . . .

3. . . . Bend over, get on his level. A dog seems to be born with the ability to sense how you feel. Show him you want to be friends and he is doing a fine job. He'll respond — fast.

SOME TIPS TO REMEMBER

Since many of the things that you have learned were learned much the way a dog has to learn, your own common sense and intuition will help you work out problems that arise in the training. A little thought, a little judgment will show you the way.

I remember while working with my first dog that I had a problem that I couldn't seem to solve. When I'd come home from work the pup was full of beans. After supper during the lessons she was sluggish and showed no enthusiasm. Why did she lose her pep? What was I doing wrong? Thinking it over for a few days, the answer finally came — don't train on a full stomach, feed the dog after school.

It is only logical that there should be no distractions when school is in session like kids playing near-by. Don't allow an audience, work alone with the pup.

Keep the lessons short, don't let the dog get bored. Don't overdo. How will you know when you're going too far? Some trainers suggest training by the clock, ten minutes. I do it by the tail. The tail is a very good indicator of a dog's attitude. A high tail means he's still with you. A low tail means he's "gazing out the window."

On some days a dog will be more receptive than on others. After ten minutes or so if he wants to keep going, if he's still enthusiastic, continue. The important thing here is to judge the dog's progress by the indicators; his tail, his enthusiasm, his response. They show you how fast you can advance your dog from lesson to lesson. As he gets older his mental endurance will increase.

Learn to anticipate what your dog is going to do. This will take a lot of the frustration out of the yard training for both of you. For example: When a pup is held by command in the SIT, STAY position, he, of course, will want to break and come to you. After he has held it for a short period, but just can't stand it any longer, he'll give a warning by a slight body movement that he is about to break. Anticipate this — command COME just before he breaks. Now he has done two things correctly instead of one thing incorrectly. The lesson continues in a happy mood.

Try to end school each day on a good note. If he's not progressing on the latest lesson to your satisfaction, the last command should be something he already knows well. Then you can ring the bell, close up school for the day, and give the pup some loving. Tomorrow is another day.

One last word — it won't be long until you both are thinking like dogs. You'll both learn how each other's cogs work, how to anticipate each other. This will have a deadly effect on you. You'll be looking at your family and friends from a little different perspective. Many times you will think the dog is almost talking to you and *you'll* have to stifle the temptation to bark back. Your everyday life can be affected. This happened to me on the first dog I trained, with rather startling results. A friend who aspires to be a writer was so intrigued that he set it all down on paper:

There are dangers in training a hunting dog that do not immediately meet the eye, and some of them may have dark social implications. A man training a dog can train himself into a different personality, and not necessarily a better one.

There is Richard Wolters of Ossining, N.Y., whose dog now appears to be training him. Wolters got himself a setter puppy and set to work to train her.

Pretty soon the puppy, then three months old, was answering voice, whistle, and hand signals in the yard. Wolters was particular about those hand signals, reasoning that the puppy might not always be able to hear him. Before the dog was five months old it would stop when he held up his hand, palm outward, and come when he dropped his hand quickly.

This is all very well, and what a dog ought to do, but a man ought not to do the same. Wolters began to have a tendency to stop when he saw an upraised hand. If somebody said the word "stay" in ordinary conversation, he got a strange urge to freeze in any position that he happened to be in at the moment.

His four-year-old daughter, Gretchen, got wind of this and one day ordered him to "sit" when he was standing over a toy fire engine. He sat compulsively.

The dog is six months old now, and finding and standing birds stylishly. Wolters would be doing the same but his nose is not good enough.

He was walking down a ramp in the Ossining railroad station last night to catch a train with Mrs. Wolters. The ramp was crowded. A local pulled in and the conductor jumped off and threw up a hand, palm outward, to signal the engineer. Wolters froze.

"What's your problem, Mac?" the man behind him asked.

"He gave the stop signal, didn't he?" Wolters demanded angrily.

"The guy ain't signaling you, stupid," the man said, and pushed by.

Wolters brooded on this on the trip into town and had got himself quieted down a little by the time he reached Grand Central. Everything might have been all right if a trainman had not swung a red lantern to his right in a signal to the engineer.

Wolters broke to his right, upsetting a little girl and crashing into a train on the far track. But what made him lose his temper was that he then looked back to see if the trainman would signal for him to quarter.

He is a chemist by education, though he no longer follows that trade, and is now trying to formulate an equation for this behavior. Mrs. Wolters, a Columbia graduate student in sociology, is even more concerned. She thinks animals may be taking over the social order.

In any case, she doesn't like her husband to respond to everybody's hand signals. Afraid he might lie down in Grand Central Station, or point sparrows in the yard. Sociology students do not like such departures from what they probably call the norm.

The dog is all right though; quite tractable and conventional. He may yet bring Wolters back, by example, to the norm.

Part II

Chapter 6

Preschool — The Five Important Weeks

The requirements for Seeing Eye Dogs are rigid. For years it was assumed that breeding was the answer to supplying puppies for this training. However, using pups from the very best stock, only 20 per cent were able to go through the training and on to become Guide Dogs for the blind. This percentage was obviously much too low, so Dr. Scott and his team of workers sought — and found the answer in a new approach to training. In a word, the new training system is acceleration.

With the new information that had come to light regarding the crucial periods in the development of the puppies, new training techniques were instigated: The different phases of a puppy's education must begin and continue without interruption in correlation with his natural mental development. It was discovered to be most important not to let training lag behind the puppy's unfolding abilities. Previously no one ever dreamed that, for example, a seven-weeks-old puppy could ever begin his official training.

When the training of the Seeing Eye Dogs began at five weeks and was carried through without interruption 90 per cent, instead of 20 per cent of the puppies went on to become Guide Dogs. This greatly exceeded their expectations for the experiments. Following the recommendations of the Hamilton Station, Guide Dogs for the Blind, Inc., reports that in actual practice, in a period of one year, they had 94 per cent success. Nine of the litters during that period under this new training regime produced 100 per cent Guide Dogs.

You have one dog. You need 100 per cent success. Success starts in preschool.

Our primary purpose of the training in this fourth critical period is to condition the puppy for learning. During these few weeks, as Dr. Scott discovered, the environment, the mild restrictions, the games, and most important, the human contact will prepare the pup for his future life; here we are building the foundations of a well-balanced dog. There are four areas of the puppy's behavior that we're interested in developing in preschool.

4. A happy puppy will play all by himself and he will give the brush-off to insecurity.

THE FOUR ASPECTS OF EARLY LEARNING
1. SECURITY

A secure pup is a happy pup. This is accomplished by having the pup live with you, providing him with all his needs, protecting him from harm, and making his new home a pleasant one. A puppy that will play by himself and not just sit and be a wallflower is secure. An emotionally secure dog will take to his lessons easily. Hunters who have what they call sensitive dogs actually have insecure dogs.

2. HUMAN CONTACT

Until he comes home with you, his main contacts have been with the bitch and his litter mates. It is essential that good rapport with people and especially with you take place during this time. A pup at this age will form natural attachments to the one who cares for him and instructs him. Emotional development of the pup is linked with his physical and mental growth. Whoever takes the place of the mother will become very important to the dog. You should be the one who feeds the puppy. This is the time to form a strong bond between dog and man. This is why many dogs left in the kennel four or five months will never develop to their full potential as hunting companions.

5. These pups became acquainted in seconds. At this age, a dog forms his strongest bond with man. Depriving a dog of this can seriously affect his ability to learn later.

6. They soon trusted each other and became fast friends. But, he got the popsicle. Dealing with people before his ways are set will lead to his being a tractable dog.

7. He sits up. He thinks he's people. At this age he'll even try to talk to you...Yes sir...

8. ... at seven-weeks-old, a puppy is unusually susceptible to environmental influences.

9. When kept in the house, dogs get more attention which is very important in the early education. They love to play. Play for a pup is the early foundation for team work . . .

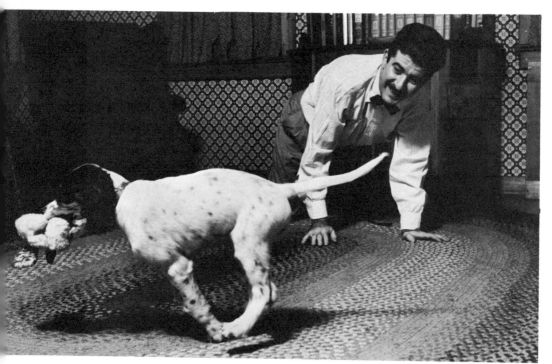

10. . . . "I said team work. You're to bring it to me!" There is never reprimand in these play games. Show pleasure when he finally brings it. It develops his willingness to please.

11. Even a grown dog needs and wants attention. If he doesn't get enough he'll come and ask for it. Dogs need companionship. A dog that learns to like affection is easier to train. His desire for affection leads to a desire to please. This is your most valuable training tool for teaching.

12. The bond between boy and dog better not get any closer. This sure is much better than his living alone in the cold kennel.

Life is not a bed of roses. The sooner he learns that, the better he'll get along both in and out of school. Being able to cope with annoying situations and not sulking will make him a cooperative student. Place him in some mildly irritating situations. He has to learn to put up with it and make the best of things. Uncooperative hunting dogs are useless, they won't hunt as partners.

LEASE & COLLAR

13. He's all dressed up, but it's a pain in the neck. Below, he solves problem by his making the best of the situation and using his time wisely. Learning early to put up with mild restrictions, not always getting his way, will make him a cooperative student.

15. He might as well get over the balkiness in kindergarten. A few minutes every day will give him the idea that life is not just eating, sleeping and playing. But don't be rough on him now, he has plenty to learn.

16. Even big dogs have to learn to put up with all kinds of annoyances: like playing house.

4. ACCEPTING RESTRICTIONS

Teach this one early and half your battle is won. All training is restrictive in nature. You as the trainer give the commands when you see fit. The dog, and especially a working dog, must do what you say when you say it. Here in preschool, early learning must include restraints, taboos, discipline, and mild punishment. The biggest training problem hunters can have is a hardheaded dog. That problem would not exist if the dog were taught at the crucial time of his development to accept discipline and restriction.

17. A barking dog may not bite, but the neighbors will. Teach the command QUIET. Firmly grab his snout, squeeze it a little and stoutly repeat the command QUIET. He is now old enough to learn simple things of life and it's vital to his mental development he be taught during this period.

18. Oh, how he wants to play, but now you've other things to do. It is better to learn now that he does things when you want,

19. Life's tough, but that's just one more big restriction around this house. You've got to learn it's like the mail. It comes every day in rain, hail, sleet, or still of night ...OUTSIDE. Remember that, OUTSIDE.

not when he wants to. If he starts to raise hell, make him wait. Do not let him learn that barking will get him off scot-free.

20. "I know it's startling, but SIT!" Simple commands can be taught to him now ...

21. ..."All the way down Puppy." We'll discuss these commands in full detail later ...

22. ..."Now you see and hear command SIT." Just wanted to show you off at 10 weeks...

23. ..."STAY, here's the hand signal." Five minutes of work he learned all of this ...

24. ...He even held STAY as I moved back. He was quite remarkable for ten weeks old. We had good rapport, any puppy near graduation from nursery school can learn all this...

LEARNING PREPARES HIM FOR HIS FUTURE

25. ...He automatically came on command. Do not overdo these lessons, especially if he is a little slow. But make him do some each day. Make a big fuss over him. He will love playing these games, so will you.

37

FUN: PRESCHOOL STUFF FOR THE HUNTING DOG

Every chance you can get, walk your dog afield. Let him learn as soon as possible that it's a big world. At first a stump or a rock might frighten him. The birds, the bees, the smells and things will give him a big charge. Plenty of loving and these exciting walks are his reward for his work at nursery school.

26. Let him explore. Take him out with you as often as possible. He'll learn to look forward to these walks. Even dark shadows are exciting and scary in the big new world.

27. A bird wing on the end of a rod and line is rather exciting for the puppy. Most new owners like to see if their new dogs will point. It's a fun game for you and the pup. If he doesn't point don't worry. It's only a game. We'll show how to teach it later.

28. "Call the gang. Wait till next fall!" This is the first time the puppy has ever seen this wing. His first point — pretty stylish. Of course he's pointing by sight not by scent.

A WORD OF WARNING

Don't overdo the training. Give the puppy a chance to rest. You are not really trying to teach him things, you are developing attitudes at this time. Of course, there are certain habits he must learn, housebreaking, quiet, and the like. On these be firm, on other things be kind and gentle. Let him learn to love you. That is more important right now than his being able to sit on command. His concentration span is short. Be alert, watch for him to tire. Of utmost importance, make this preschool experience fun.

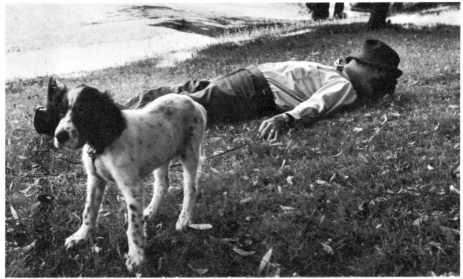

29. Beware. Don't overdo.

Chapter 7

The Puppy Goes to School

The first weeks of preschool are over. The hunting puppy is now twelve weeks old. At the beginning of the last chapter you were told that 90 per cent of the well-bred puppies whose training was started at five weeks became Seeing Eye dogs. If you read that sentence over about starting the training you will see that it includes the phrase "without interruption." If at the end of the preschool training (age twelve weeks) the lessons stopped and the dog lived again in a kennel for a period of only two weeks, the research showed only 57 per cent went on to become useful Guide Dogs. If the formal lessons and the human contact were stopped for three weeks, only 30 per cent became Seeing Eye Dogs.

These following formal lessons will be fully successful because your puppy has had the informal preschool training we have just gone through.

This is the fifth critical period, the last phase of the puppy's mental development. Now the real work begins. The play lessons end.

We are going to teach the basic commands on the conscious level. On the unconscious level we are going to prepare the dog for hunting. Then we will also teach some commands for convenience, so the two of you can live together — each in his place. There will be no rolling over, playing dead, saying prayers, begging, and so forth. That stuff is for the cocktail party. The only cocktail this dog will see is going to be in the field. Don't clutter up his brain with any useless nonsense. At six months we're going to have you hunting with him.

Your pup is three months old. In two hours or so of the formal schooling, that is, two weeks of ten-minutes-a-day lessons, your pup will have learned SIT, STAY, COME, WHOA, HEEL, KENNEL, NO, and DOWN.

THE BASIC COMMANDS: SIT — STAY — COME — WHOA

The four basic commands are essential. The last two, COME and WHOA, are so important that if a dog had good hunting instincts and knew only these two commands he would make a gun dog. We will teach these, however, as part of a series. Here's why. First teach SIT. That gives you control of the training situation. Then teach STAY. This gives you the flexibility needed in the teaching situation. You now can leave the dog, go to the other side of the classroom, whether it's your yard or living room and teach the next command — COME. Once these are cemented in the think tank, teach WHOA. Let's show you how we go about it.

SIT

The dog is first taught this command on a leash. This gives you control since a leash to a dog means restraint. After the second lesson you can start doing this without the leash. When he falters, and he will, don't scold him — just put him back on the leash. He learns in this way that if he does not do what you say, back on the leash he goes and then you can *make* him do it. Right from the beginning this will help establish who is boss. After he has learned the command, by voice, introduce the first hand signal.

30. Walk the dog briskly on a short leash held in your left hand...

SIT, TAKE A LOAD OFF YOUR FEET, RIGHT NOW

31. ...Switch the leash to your right hand. Give the command SIT. Then the left hand starts to push down on his hindquarters...

32. ...Right hand pulls his head up, left forces him to ground. All the way down. At first he'll fight this but keep repeating it...

33. ...The head is held up so he won't lie down. Praise him. As soon as he sits down without the help of your pushing hand...

34. ...remove the leash. Now, step ahead of him just before you give command SIT. Show him hand signal—extended finger.

35. Surprise him every once in a while, try it on him when he is playing. Reinforce the voice command with hand signal. In a few weeks he'll sit when he sees the extended finger go down. Now he is learning to obey by sight or sound. The use of the hand signal is very important from the beginning, although later we may find no need for him to sit by hand. He learns to obey the hand signals, which become extensive later.

36. Command STAY. Give the hand signal immediately. Hold him in place on a short leash...

37. ... Repeat STAY. Slowly walk in front of him. Show the hand signal. Repeat STAY. Hold him in place ...

38. ..."Stop mugging the camera! Pay attention to hand signal as I move saying . .

41. By the third lesson you will be doing all this without the leash. If he falters, put him back on. From the beginning teach him that the leash means you are in control.

STAY, STAY..STAY...STAY....

The SIT, STAY command may save your dog's life someday. Or, it might just make life a little easier for you. When you walk the dog to the drugstore for those aspirins, a SIT, STAY command will keep him out of some kid's ice cream cone. There will be many occasions even on hunting trips when you will want to keep the dog out of the way. You can't teach a dog COME if he's sitting at your heels. STAY gives you the opportunity to set up the situation for future lessons. Here's how we do it. Put the pup back on the leash. Make sure all your body motions are slow and deliberate.

39. ...STAY. That's better." Now you gradually release the pressure on the dog's collar. Start to . . . . . .

40. ...slowly move backwards. Repeat the command at every step. Push the signaling hand toward him, palm out. Most important, be slow and deliberate.

42. When you think he has this, walk away, watching him over your shoulder. Continually maintain the hand signal and repeat the vocal command. If he falters, take him back to where he was, start over. In two weeks you'll be able to leave the yard, he'll stay.

COME, LEARN IT NOW — IF YOU DON'T!!

A *most* important command for the field. This is going to be your control of the dog's range for hunting. Right now we are interested in the elementary classroom lesson. Later we'll discuss COME as applied to the field; here is where this system makes a major departure from other training systems.

There are a number of ways to teach COME. It is very easy. One thing he has to learn, you must be *obeyed immediately*. Not tomorrow, not next week, but *right now*.

This command is going to be taught so that the dog will learn to respond to it by means of three signals: the voice command COME, the whistle — two short blasts, the hand signal — dropping of the hand toward the ground from the upraised *stay* signal.

I have often been asked why I teach the command COME by the hand signal. There are two good reasons. One, there is nothing worse than hunting with a guy who is calling his dog or blowing a whistle all day. On many occasions your dog will look back to check on you. The drop of the hand will bring him in if you wish. The second reason is the most important, getting the dog in the habit of checking back with you. This will be useful in teaching the dog to hunt within range.

I have never seen a dog that wouldn't eagerly respond to this. They learn this command in a couple of lessons. In a few weeks they will come

44. Command SIT, STAY. Being away from him, you can now teach the command COME... **45.** ...Let him hear it! Simultaneously drop the hand, blast twice on your whistle. It'll get him up . . . . .

46. . . . If not, but in either case, turn and run like hell away from him, clapping your hands. He'll come a-running to get to you. It's great sport for him and he's learning.

by any one of the three signals. If for any reason something goes wrong here, there is another method to fall back on. It has been used by trainers for generations. Don't use it unless you have to. Put the dog back on the leash. Command SIT, STAY. Walk backward to the end of the leash. If you like, you can tie a piece of rope on it to make it longer. Command COME, drop your hand from the upheld position, blow the whistle. Give the leash a little jerk and with it draw the dog toward you. This will display to the dog what is expected.

Picture 47 will show why I do not like this system. The dog shows no enthusiasm. If you do use this procedure to teach *Come*, as soon as you think the dog knows what the command means, take him off the leash.

47. On a leash he's forced to learn what the command COME means. He knows he'll be pulled if he doesn't come. The dog will learn this way, but he won't be happy about it.

WHOA — DROP THE DISHES AND STOP — RIGHT NOW

A dog's natural instinct is to rush in and grab a bird. The pointing dogs, through generations of training, have been bred to point or set game. This, however, is contrary to their basic instinct. The intoxicating scent of game is to a dog what perfume is to a man — he wants it — badly. Unfortunately for the dog he is not hunting for himself. You are the hunter, his job is to find the game and signal you. When he does find it he is taught to hold and not flush the bird. The signal that he gives is the rigid position caused by the nervous excitement. Every fiber of the animal is called upon to prepare for the spring. Thus the point. Often puppies on their first point will almost fall over, they are shaking so hard. The command WHOA is the most important hunting command. All the rest are for control or convenience. If it takes a dog three seconds to stop dead in his tracks on command WHOA, it may be too late — the bird flushes. There can be no compromise on this part of your contract. Either he's in business for himself, or he respects the partnership and waits for you.

The point seldom happens like something dropping out of the blue. At the first inkling of scent the dog will "make game." This is very easy to recognize. No matter how tired the dog is he will shift to high gear. His tail will start to go in a circle so fast that if he had wings, he'd fly. He'll lift his head and use the wind to get direction. As the scent increases he'll settle in and prepare for the spring or point. Like many setters, Beau has a great habit. He goes like ninety while making game. Then, when the scent is strong he will go up on point. But when I reach him, if his tail is moving very slowly from side to side, it means that he has not pinpointed the exact location of the bird, or that the bird might be running. I do not go in then to flush the bird, I tell him to GO IN — EEEZY. Now, when he goes on point and has relocated the bird, he's as solid as a rock. The tail is high and rigid. I whisper command WHOA just to reassure, walk in, and in my usual way, flush the bird and miss it. Thank goodness that in our business contract I was smart enough to insist on being treasurer of our outfit or I'd never get paid.

WHOA is taught in many ways by different trainers. First, I would like to discuss their systems. One technique is to teach the command at meal-time to a pup that has just been weaned. Hold the pup a few feet from his dish and give the WHOA command several times. Stroke him gently as you do this. When he is released you command GO IN. This system has always produced bad results for me — an eating problem.

Another way is to attach a rope on a pulley to a stake. You have the dog SIT, STAY with the pulley at his back. Then you command COME. As he does you pay out rope. Command WHOA, jerk the dog to a stop with the rope. This system is too complicated for me and my dogs have been too smart. They obey if there is a stake around.

My system is flexible. You do not need a construction crew to set up the apparatus. It works best on young dogs, and a dog should be young when he learns this. I'll teach WHOA to a dog in five minutes if he has been pre-pared for it. The preparations are the last three commands you have taught: SIT, STAY, COME. The hand signal for STAY is of vital importance here. The dog is ready to learn WHOA as soon as he will STAY on hand signal alone and COME on command. When he has this down pat, my system is — *scare hell out of the dog.*

Put the pup in the SIT STAY position. Walk a good distance away from him . . . Command COME. Run like hell away from him . . . Make him get up steam. Then reverse your field. Turn, run at the dog. Shout WHOA. Thrust the hand up in the STAY hand signal like a traffic cop. Jump in the air at him. *Do it with gusto.* You'll look so foolish doing it that he'll stop.

48. WHOA! This crazy action done with gusto would stop anything. This method will teach the command almost instantly. Remember, have him responding well to the previous commands, especially STAY, by hand signal. At first he may seem confused — no wonder.

I'm sure at this point he will wonder how he ever got tangled in business with such a crazy guy, but he'll remember the command.

As you see you are working this command backward. The first three in this series were taught by voice. The supporting commands (hand and whistle) were learned by association. Here the supporting signal is the voice. The dog learned WHOA by the crazy hand signal. Now we have to reverse it. In the field this command will only be given by voice. To teach

49. Gradually reduce the violent hand signal. Let the voice command WHOA take over. In the field he will be expected to respond instantly to this command, by voice only.

WHOA by the voice command, put the dog back into SIT STAY. Command COME. When he gets halfway to you, command WHOA firmly. Give the hand signal for STAY but without gusto. Repeat this, diminishing the vehemence of the hand signal.

When the pup has learned this, start giving the command by voice only. This whole procedure with a four-month-old pup will be learned in about a week.

Do not use this command for any purpose other than when game is involved or you think game is involved. This is to stop your dog, to steady him on point, or when he's about to point. This command prevents him from flushing the bird. The command is also used to teach him to honor the point of another dog. When you want to stop the dog on occasions when game is not involved command SIT.

Whether you are training in your living room or an open field, spring this command on your dog, but not too often. Never let him anticipate the command. Throughout this training don't worry if the dog sits when he stops. He's to learn the command means stop, but he won't know why yet. We will teach him why in a later lesson with the fly rod and the wing.

You can loose control of your dog when the WHOA command is given under the intoxicating influence of game scent. But, the rod and wing will have taught him the why of the command, and he'll know what you expect of him. In the last chapter, when we take the dog hunting, we will show how to teach him that we mean business on this command. WHOA means — *Drop the dishes and stop* — *right now!*

NO, IT MEANS WHAT IT SAYS — NO

There is really no formal lesson here. The dog has heard this from the second hour he has been in the home with you. Just make sure it's firm. I won't take the time here to tell you just when you will use this command, but it will be often. Accept no compromise here.

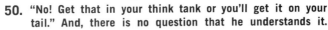

50. "No! Get that in your think tank or you'll get it on your tail." And, there is no question that he understands it.

51. On a short leash command HEEL, slap your leg. If he is rampant let him go . . .

52. . . . to the end of the leash. He'll jam up on it. Don't yank him back. Hold him right there . . .

53. . . . You move up to him taking in line. Start over, slap your leg, give command HEEL. Your leg slap is his hand signal.

54. Don't drag the lagging dog forward. Slap your leg, command HEEL, wait for him to walk up. Talk gently to him and start all over on a short leash.

HEEL

This is for both safety and convenience. If you are a right-handed shooter the dog should always be on your left side.

Having your dog at your side while walking is desirable for obvious reasons. A dog on leash that always wants to be out in front leading the band is a pain in the neck. The way to cure this pain is to yank him, give him the pain in the neck. But, the situation should not be allowed to get this far out of hand. If he's trained correctly, he'll walk in step.

In preschool the pup learned to put up with the collar and leash. In four or five formal lessons he should learn to heel. Put the dog in the SIT STAY position. Don't forget, whenever you are teaching new commands, run through some of the old ones first. This is to get the dog responding to you.

55. The get-in-the-way walker learns to stay on his own feet, on his own sidewalk, after a few kicks. Never walk out of his way, he'll learn his place very soon.

56. The finishing touches are put on with use of a stick. This holds him in his place. When you feel he knows what's expected, remove the leash and try it.

57. For safety, I always make a dog sit before we cross the street. He too, learns to watch out for crazy drivers.

58. For safety in the field, the dog is on one side and the gun is on the other.

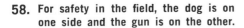

KENNEL

It takes a matter of minutes to teach this to a pup. Command SIT STAY in front of the kennel door. Point, command KENNEL. If he does not go in, shove him in. The second time he'll go in. This eleven-week pup learned the command in two minutes.

Dogs are a lot cleaner in the house than a lot of people I know, but it's hard to convince motel and hotel operators. On hunting trips the dog has to learn to live in the car. The Kennel Aire makes a fine place for the dog to live. While travelling he can see everything that's going on, and driving is easier, you can see through the cage. At night throw a cover over the kennel. It doesn't make any difference how cold it gets, the area is small enough that his body heat warms the whole cage.

Start a pup off in a cage and he will soon know that's his place in the car. Of course he's not going to like being left alone. When he's about four months old start taking him to parties, that is, you go to the party and the dog stays locked in the car. Don't do this at home, he won't understand. In slow steps get him used to the idea. At first he'll bark his head off. You've put him in this situation and he'll find the solution eventually — sleep. Don't go to the car to shush him. He'll think that barking makes you come, that's what he wants. Gradually increase the length of time, and when you go on the first hunting trip he'll be quieter in the car than those people supposedly sleeping in the next room.

59. Command KENNEL. "That's your home...   **60.** ...and this is it when we go hunting."

DOWN

This is something I never teach a dog. If he wants to show he likes me by jumping up, I'm willing to pay for a cleaning bill if this makes him happy. But, just to be a good citizen he must learn not to do it to others. I have my wife teach this one.

With a small pup, the palm in the nose will do the trick. Don't do the bit about stepping on the dog's hind feet when he jumps up. First, it's hard to do, second, a shoe can damage a paw.

As you may have noticed we have not taught the dog to lie down. We won't . . . there's no need for it. If he sits, that's enough. There is no place for the command in hunting or as a building block in training. So, if he wants to lie down when he is tired, that's his business.

61. A knee from underneath is quite a surprise. He expected a pat. When he jumps up, bring up the knee, strike him an easy blow in the chest. Grab his front paws, command DOWN. Throw him off.

Chapter 8

Direction, Range, Control — Step by Step

No one part of a dog's training is separate from another. All facets of the training are woven together like a piece of cloth. We're hoping that the final design will be a nice hunting motif. While the yard training is going on, work should be started in the field. For those readers who have acreage at their disposal this is fine. I haven't — so I do my training in a park or an open lot.

More dogs are ruined during this part of the training than at any other. At this point let's state our purpose once again. Then you will see why our step by step plan is necessary.

We're not training a field trial dog — we want a gun dog. The difference here is that we want our dog to stay under control in range. It does not dampen the dog's enthusiasm to hunt within one hundred yards of you. You're going to save much training time having your dog hunt close. It's only natural that you can't make corrections in the field if your dog is half-way down the valley. Even more important, the dog is to learn that he is hunting for you, not for himself. This is essential.

Our system of teaching direction, range, and control will be a reverse of other training methods. Instead of having the young dog running hell bent all over the countryside to encourage his desire to hunt and then hope to get control later, we are going to keep the dog in so you will know where he is and what he's doing.

The first year he hunts close so that he can learn what is expected of him. Once he knows we'll increase his range. It is easier to increase a dog's range than it is to curb a dog that is used to going out as far as he pleases.

Remember, this is your all-around dog. He is not a specialist. He won't cover the ground like a wide-ranging quail dog when you have him down South, but, if he did and you put him on grouse up North, the birds would make fools of both of you.

When I gave my son his first bicycle he was allowed to ride only on the street in front of the house. As I saw that he knew how to handle himself, his range was increased.

I had to have control over my boy for this plan to work. You are going to have to have control over your dog. When that whistle blows, he comes — or else. Having the dog work close as a puppy will prevent him from falling into the useless habit of going off for himself — a natural instinct. You can't prevent him from doing it by calling him to your study and having a discussion about it as you can with your boy. *You will have to show him*. With a little firmness he will know he can't get away. The dog will keep glancing back over his shoulder, checking with you. Now he has the idea — you are calling the signals.

Here's what you can expect from the coming lessons: This is part of the unconscious learning that we've talked about. First, we teach the puppy to take his correct place, in front of the hunter. He will learn this by habit. If you start your puppy at a very young age, he'll have a strong desire to stay very close to you. We'll take advantage of this, and on the first few walks teach him this place in the field.

Next, we'll teach him to hunt the area. As he develops more boldness and wanders farther away from you, but still has need to be near you, we teach him how to hunt or quarter.

We'll wind up by having him do all this by hand signal alone. Having implanted the habit of being in the right place and doing the right thing early in his training, before he's had an opportunity to learn anything else, he'll be 'way ahead of the game. He'll have nothing to unlearn. And the best part of this system is that he has learned without knowing it.

THE HUNTING DOG'S PLACE

Remember back in preschool the puppy was taken out into the field just to teach him it was a big world. More often than not the puppy at first will not want to be even a foot away from you in the new, big, strange surroundings. This early we start to teach the puppy his place when he goes into the field with you. Lift your heels when he gets too close, gently bump him in the chin. This will teach him to keep his distance.

From now on whenever you take him for a run whether it be in the field or a park, walk him to the center of the area on a leash. Now if he wants to get behind you, turn around. Now he's in front of you. Wherever he goes, face him.

62. "Walk on your feet, not mine." He'll want to be very close to you. He'll have to learn to get off your heels. Lift your foot, clip him gently in the jaw. He'll stay back . . .

63. ...When he learns to stay away, even if it's a few feet, turn around, face him...

64. ...Now he's in front. Never let him behind you again. Always turn facing him...

65. ... unconsciously, in a few outings, he will learn without any effort on your part that his place on walks is in front of you.

ZIGZAG — A CROOKED LINE WITH DIRECTION

Now he's getting bolder and is always out front. But, he's still not bold enough to run off. He wants to have you in sight. Wherever you go he will want to go. We will use this to our advantage and zigzag across the field. When you zig, he will zig. When you zag, he'll want to be with you, so he'll zag. You are both covering the area that has to be hunted. He is learning a pattern and the appropriate hand signals at the same time.

Walk briskly while doing this — a dog likes to move when out for a run.

After a bold young dog learns this he might have a tendency to run off in familiar territory. A smart dog will turn familiar terrain into his own back yard. Take such a dog to a new area. He won't be so bold.

In this sequence of pictures, the flagpole is your reference point to show how to cover the area.

66. Now that he has learned that his place will be in front of the hunter at all times . . .

67. . . . start in the middle of the field. Go any direction. Then change your course, he'll . . .

68. . . . change his, knowing he is to be in front. When you change course give a YIP or a single whistle blast for attention. Show him the hand signal for the new direction . . .

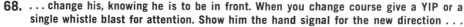

69. ... You'll soon be able to turn, say nothing, give no signal and he'll fall in place ...

70. ... If he putters, command GO ON. This is a new command. He'll learn to keep moving ...

71. ... In a milder tone of voice repeat the GO ON command when he is going on. This will show him further what you want and what the command means. He'll catch on fast ...

72. ... In a week or so he will learn these two commands, GO ON and the direction signal ...

73. ... The zigzag method is easy on you and on the dog. By repetition he is learning to quarter. Of course, this is not your hunting pattern, but it will be his in the field.

A STRAIGHT LINE WILL TEACH HIM TO QUARTER

This lesson is a continuation of the last one. It will reinforce the learning of direction by hand signal and will give the dog his first lessons in quartering. Quartering is the hunting pattern the dog makes as he ranges back and forth in front of you. This is the area the dog will hunt.

By repeating the hand signals each time you zig or zag the dog learns to associate the signal with the new direction. You can test to see if he's getting the idea of going in the desired direction by signal. If he is not responding, continue the zigzag with the appropriate signal. Gradually reduce the distance you walk each time you take a new direction. He will be learning to take his cue from your hand signal. The hand signal will take on more importance, and you will have reduced the zigzag to the point where you will be walking a straight line and the dog will be responding entirely to hand signals.

74. Now that he knows what his hunting pattern is, he has to learn to do it on his own . .

75. ... Gradually make your zigzag pattern smaller and smaller, until you are walking in a straight line. If he goes off too far on a cast, bring him back with the whistle . . .

76. . . . Be consistent with the pattern, soon he will be checking to see if he is right . . .

77. . . . Lean your body into hand directional signals, even exaggerate them a little bit . . .

78. . . . From what was once just a desire to be with you, he has learned how to quarter . . .

79. . . . Just make sure he's learned, send him back over the same ground. He should respond.

80. Attention. He sees signal, hears whistle. 81. Left

LEAD HIM IN THE FIELD — BY THE HAND

84. If he doesn't know what you want by one blast, follow it immediately with command SIT, STAY ...

85. ... Next time he sits on ATTENTION. Command fast with a directional hand signal. Command GO ON ...

82. Right

83. Confused! Don't hide signals, wrong hand.

What has been taught in the yard and the park now has to be carried over into the field. With the new smell and the big world around him we will need a new command — ATTENTION. This will be one blast on the whistle. If you have trouble with this and he doesn't understand, wait until he is coming toward you, blast once, command SIT. That will keep him from thinking one blast means COME. This will let him know you want him to do something. Immediately send him off with a direction signal. Repeat this situation, substitute different direction signals for SIT. Shortly SIT will not be necessary.

86. . . . Get him going in both directions. This all gets to be a game. It'll pay off hunting.

87. Run at him, give overhand throw signal. Command GO ON in a rousing voice...

88. ... Keep running towards him, repeating signal with gusto, shouting GO ON...

LETTING GO OF THE APRON STRINGS

Increasing the dog's hunting range is accomplished by his learning another hand signal. For the one-dog man this is to be taught after the dog has hunted one season in close to you, but I'm including it here because it is a hand signal. It's out of sequence, but it's better to explain it while you are learning how to teach signals. Let me reemphasize here the importance of the dog hunting close enough to you the first year, so that you will be able to correct and control him. Otherwise, your dog will be off hunting for himself, and your hunting companions will also be off hunting by themselves, and you will be left holding the empty bag.

89. ... He'll turn and run. He may be muttering to himself the first few times he sees your crazy act, but soon he will be doing this when he sees just the overhand throw signal.

Teaching a dog to increase his range or hunt wide at this age is contrary to the methods used by other trainers. This is usually one of the first things they like to have their dogs do. That's where I disagree with the field trial method of training. They argue that it instills and shows boldness and spirit. A bold spirited dog bumping birds out of shotgun range can be mighty exasperating to a hunting party. Later we will show you how to correct the young dog when he bumps or flushes a bird that he should have pointed, but in order to make the correction you are going to have to be near your dog.

There's another reason trainers like their dogs to hunt wide at a young age. They feel that if the dog does not learn this early in life he never will learn it. They are absolutely right — *if* the dog was not started in his training at the correct age. Dr. Scott's experiments at Hamilton Station have shown that dogs who have had the advantage of preschool training can always be taught. If the dog learned to learn in preschool (seven to twelve weeks of age) he can continue to learn new things throughout his life. So, to my way of thinking, it's better for the hunter to postpone increasing the range. This way he can have more control during early training in the field. Teach first things first, and you will speed up the training job.

How do we teach a dog to increase his range? What is the hand signal? Simple. Just play like you're a baseball pitcher. When the dog starts to swing in toward you on a cast, run at him. Make an overhand motion at him just like the one the pitcher makes when he is throwing the ball. At the same time command in a rousing voice, GO ON — GO ON. If he does not get the idea, a handful of pebbles will help the situation. Keep running at him, keep repeating the command.

OBEY THE WHISTLE OR PAY THE FINE

There is nothing worse than hunting with a fellow that blows his whistle all day, getting no response from his dog. I'm proud to have been able to write that sentence in such quiet mild language. Both hunter and dog should be thrashed. The whistle is an important control in the field. I use two short blasts — that means COME. One of my hunting cronies uses three blasts. It's better to train dogs that are going to work together to respond to different signals. This is less confusing to them. The whistle should be used sparingly.

We have seen how the dog has learned to know his place in the field. As he progresses in these hand signal lessons, you will see that fewer and fewer directions have to be given him. He will learn the pattern of what is expected of him, his instincts and hunting desire teach him the rest. It's the whistle that will be your over-all control of the situation. The dog's desires and instincts have to be curbed to some extent. The dog will be carried away by the excitement of the hunt. That's natural, but restraint is important, a part of life, as even every child must learn. We prepared the puppy to accept restraint as a way of life. Now we must make sure the dog doesn't lose this habit. We have taught the dog COME by three commands; the important command in the field will be the whistle. A good blast can be heard at least a quarter of a mile away, and a five-month-old pup should know what to do and respond smartly. If not, be prepared to show him your muscle.

Don't tell me your dog is too sensitive to learn this. Don't tell me you don't want to break the dog's spirit. Every decent hunting dog will try you to see how much he can get away with. Show him from the beginning who is boss.

There are many ways to teach this. I use two methods, depending upon the situation. Before I discuss mine, I'll tell you about two other techniques. The first is the check cord. The idea here is to grab the fifty-foot rope and yank it as you blow the whistle, pulling the dog in to you. A dog will soon learn to respond to this — if he is on a cord. He may also learn that you can't do a damn thing about it when he is not on the cord. Besides, a fifty-foot cord is just not long enough. If you can get within fifty feet of a dog, you won't need to blow your whistle in normal hunting situations.

Then there's another system, in which I haven't any faith. I saw an old-timer use this method, but I don't quite follow the logic of it. When his dog didn't respond to the whistle he ran after him, put a light load of shot in the gun, and, from a good distance, took a crack at the dog. The dog ran off yelping and the trainer came back to us alone. He must have noticed the expression on my face. He said, "Peppered his ass with some lead. That'll teach him to come back next time." I thought to myself, but what about this time? What does the guy think the dog is going to learn about the sound of a gun going off?

Here are my two methods; which one I use depends on the circumstances. One method; I teach the dog to come on whistle. The other, the dog teaches himself. A word of warning here. If the dog responds, but not as quickly as you'd like, when he finally does come in to you don't reprimand him. He has done what you asked of him. He has just taken his good old time in doing it. He won't understand you if you spank him.

90. Blast twice. He's got to learn if he disobeys . . .

91. . . . Wait a minute. Try to figure where he went. If he doesn't . . .

92. . . . come, blast again. If he doesn't respond, two things you can do.

GO AFTER HIM — TEACH HIM WHAT YOU WANT

93. First decide if you can get to your dog. If so, go to him, don't wait for him to come to you in his own sweet time. A young dog is excited and raring to go . . .

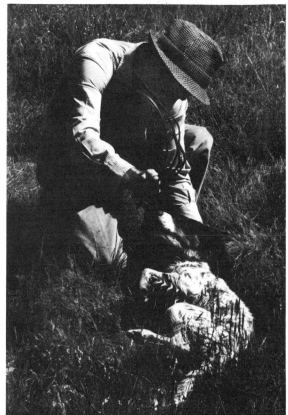

94. . . . but teach him he has to obey the whistle. Whip him until he yelps once, the same time blast twice, shout COME. Talk rough . . .

95. ... Soften the tone of your voice, then command GO ON. You can see he understands he did wrong...

96. ... When he gets out a good way, blast the COME signal ...

97. ... If he doesn't come go after him, whip him again. Most likely this will not be necessary. When he comes in to you make a fuss over him. Talk nicely, (below) tell him he's a good boy. Always end rough sessions on a friendly note. Turn page for another method.

OR...HIDE, LET HIM TEACH HIMSELF WHAT YOU WANT

99. Hide if he decides not to come in to the whistle. When he . . .

100. . . . is ready he will come looking for you and will be upset to find that you're not around. Maybe you have gone home and . . .

101. . . . left him without a home, no friends . . . **102.** . . . His whole desire now is to find you . . .

103. . . . He'll get frantic but he has no one to blame but himself. Next time he'll obey . . .

104. ... When he does track you down, he'll be happy to see you and expect you to be happy too. But, just ignore him ...

105. ... He wants to be in your good grace and he is trying to get your attention. The emotional impact will teach him to come the next time he hears a whistle.

Chapter 9

Upland Game — Fly Rod on Wing

As a young pup I didn't want to learn Shakespeare — I learned more serious poetry like:

> It is spring
> The boid is on the wing.
> Oh, how absoid,
> The wing is on the boid!

Beau, as you will see in the pictures has learned some strange things about the "boid":

> Fall or spring
> The boid is on the wing.
> How absoid bigawd
> The wing is on the rod!

In the opening chapter we talked about training tools as time and money savers. The most important one is the fishing rod with a bird wing attached to the line. In the preschool chapter we showed how the rod and wing were used as fun. Every dog owner wants to see if the puppy will point. This is not indicative of the puppy's future. But, I absolutely disagree with trainers who say that this is merely amusement for the puppy and the owner.

The puppy has to be prepared for this tool. This training method is only for amusement until the puppy has been taught the command *Whoa*. I might add here, that later we will show how the rod and wing are used to help introduce a dog to the gun, to honor another dog's point, to swim and to fetch in water.

I contend that the only reason this training method has never been presented, or as far as I know, thought out in its entirety, is because it was never needed before. Necessity is the mother of invention. Until the 1950's, when upland bird hunting practically became a mass sport, there was plenty of land and game around to train dogs, but now it would be just too damn expensive and take too long to teach a dog all he has to know about live birds. Don't misunderstand me. I am not saying that I can teach my dog to hunt in my back yard, but what I can do is teach him the commands and set up problems similar to those in the field, so that he will learn what is expected of him, and this mockup training will be transferred to birds later.

Let me put it this way. It took me four years in college to learn chemistry. The first day on the job, with my hands clutching my hot degree, I received my first blow when my boss told me it would take a year to train me as a chemist. College, he went on to say, taught me only the language of my profession. Without that, it would take years to train me and money and time are important to industry. They wouldn't have bothered if I hadn't had a thorough schooling.

Similarly, it's an economy to put the hunting dog through college to prepare him for his job in life — hunting. This preconditioning is going to put the dog 'way ahead; and the value of this rod and wing training will be measured by the ultimate rule of thumb: results.

WHAT ARE WE GOING TO TEACH WITH THE ROD AND WING?

He's going to learn twelve things that will stand him in good stead on live birds. He'll learn what is expected of him and what he can expect of you. Of course, later he'll have to transfer all he learns to the conditions in the field. Live birds will excite him, but his schooling will keep him under control, and he will know what to do. Here they are:

1. If he rushes or bolts in on a bird, he loses it.
2. To point.
3. *WHOA* — the first practical use of the command.
4. Class on point.
5. A new command, *MOVE IN — EEEZY* and reinforce *WHOA.*
6. The hunter moves ahead of the dog on point — the dog holds.
7. Hunters coming up on him while he's on point can approach from any direction without disturbing him.
8. To find a moving bird — with caution.
9. To stalk a moving bird.

and in later chapters:

10. To learn to swim and fetch in water.
11. The place of the gun in the field.
12. To back point or honor a dog already on point.

HOW DO WE TEACH ALL THIS?

A bird wing is attached to a rod and fishing line. I usually save the wings from game I shoot for this purpose, but a chicken wing from a live poultry store will do the trick. About eight feet of fishing line will give you enough length to cast the wing. If it is too long you can't control it fast enough.

Start him on this when he is a puppy, as soon as he has learned WHOA. Cast the wing in the air. That is usually enough to get a dog started. If he doesn't chase it, let it land. Most likely he'll pounce on it. If he seems reluctant, twitch it along the ground in front of him. Be ready to pick it up. In no time at all he'll be digging up the lawn.

It's hard to say what the duration of these lessons should be. I've never yet seen a dog that wanted to quit playing this game.

If your dog should show lack of interest, put the contraption away. Try him the next day. Make the motions of the feathers enticing. When he shows curiosity let him catch it a few times to whet his interest. Let him chase. When his tongue is hanging down to his knees, you have him *READY*.

106. Beau will sit and wait almost pleading for someone to swing the rod and fly the bird

107. Just to show how easy it is going to be, we taught this ten-week-old puppy to point . . .

108. ... We even made a few corrections. Turn the page to see how we teach this to a dog ...

MAKING A POINT WITH A CHASING FOOL

Tiring him out is the key to this lesson, and besides, he is learning a very important fact: he can't catch game by chasing and bolting at it. Of course he could learn this in an open field by chasing songbirds. But, unlike the songbird he chases, our bird is still around. Taking advantage of this in this controlled lesson we will teach him to point if he's reluctant to point naturally. The dog's pointing is a form of stalking. When he is sufficiently tired of chasing around, he will change his tactics and stalk — thus, the first point. Gently command WHOA when this happens. He will want to rush in, but the *STOP* command holds him. Quietly repeat the command and he'll stretch forward trying to both bolt and stop at the same time — a stanch point. This is the first practical experience for the WHOA command. WHOA is now associated with the point, its main use in the field.

109. Get him chasing the bird wing attached to the fishing rod. Swing it in the air . . .

110. . . . Tantalize him. Do not let him catch it, but do make him want it oh so badly that he'll chase . . .

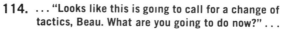

111. . . . Keep racing him until he's exhausted. He'll see that's not the way to get it . . .

112. . . . Twitch the wing along the ground. Get him excited. Don't let him rest. Just keep him going . . .

113. . . . Hell, this is lots of fun! This is the last burst of energy in him to get it . . .

114. . . . "Looks like this is going to call for a change of tactics, Beau. What are you going to do now?" . . .

115. . . . He tries to sneak in instead of chase. The point starts.
Now gently say WHOA. This creates a problem for him . . .

116. . . . He wants to go in and get the bird, but he has heard the command WHOA and now
must stay. So he tried to do both at same time—he stretches. A perfect point is made.

NOW FOR SOME ABERCROMBIE & FITCH FORM

Style or class depends on the dog; some need no correction, some point with their tail down, some from a crouch, and some without enthusiasm. Now, you have a technique where you can put your dog on point at will. You can prevent faulty habits or by repeated correction, teach him to point with style. While you are making these corrections, WHOA him in a soft voice. WHOA starts to mean more than stop — now it also means a position.

117. Teach him to lean forward by pushing him forward. This will put tension in his point.

118. Lift him by the tail, put his legs down, firmly set them. This in no way bothers him.

119. Let him fight the pressure of your leg. He keeps a point.

120. Gently WHOA him. Get the tail up. Stroke him, show him that's the position you want.

121. Put him on point. Command WHOA. Repeat command, he's steady...

122. ...Put down the fly rod. Repeat the command WHOA. He'll hold it...

123. ...Slowly move back. WHOA him, let him know you're still around.

HOW LONG IS A POINT?

In the field, a dog may be required to stay on point a considerable length of time waiting for you to reach him. We can get him used to this in the back yard.

124. . . . If he goes to move in, caution him with a WHOA. You can leave, he hasn't moved a muscle, he won't.

125. Fly wing. Get him on point a good distance from bird. WHOA him with hand and voice...

126. ...Command GO IN, EEEZY. Move in yourself. Show him hand signal. If he doesn't...

127. ...stalk with you, you move ahead, repeat command. When he joins you, WHOA him...

128. ...Soon you'll be able to take him in inches at a time with command GO IN EEEZY...

129. ... WHOA him by voice and supporting hand signal. Make sure he's staunch then ...

130. ... start to move ahead of the dog. Don't do this part until he knows GO IN EEEZY ...

EEEZY DOES IT — LET'S NOT BREAK THE EGGS

Now the dog is on point, but in the field a bird may run, or the dog may have gotten the scent from a distance and has not jammed up in a hard point. He has to learn to relocate, to move in with caution. Use a slow soft voice in this lesson. To make a dog creep in "on eggs," your voice and actions must be slow and easy. Sharp fast commands produce sharp fast action. We are going to teach the dog two things here: first, the command GO IN — EEEZY, second, that the dog holds on point while the hunter moves in ahead to flush the bird. It's not the dog's job to get the bird — it's yours.

131. ... He's ready for the next step. Use firmer voice and hand signal. Hold him on point by command. With smooth, slow motions move ahead. Fast jerking motions might cause him to break. He has to learn that hunter goes in to flush birds—he holds.

NOW WHO'S DOING THE CHASING?

Under ideal hunting conditions the hunter is supposed to come up behind a dog on point. This can't always be the case. I saw a young dog hunt quail beautifully down South. He held twenty birds . . . busted four. Talking it over at the end of the day, someone remembered that all the birds he rushed were approached by the hunter so that the dog on point could see him coming. This lesson, walking around the dog on point, will get him used to the idea that he can be approached from any direction and still do his job — HOLD THE BIRD.

132. You can put him on point at will. From the very beginning he loves to do it. He has to learn to mind his business while you do yours. Command WHOA. Repeat command as you walk around him. Get him used to being approached from any angle.

137. Get him on good staunch point. Get set and then flip the wing over his head . . .

138. . . . "Glory be where's your tail?" He's afraid to move, afraid he'll bust the bird.

PUTTING THE STALK ON A BIRD'S TAIL

I really feel that a dog is born with the knowledge to stalk. But, what we can do under these controlled conditions is develop the trait. He knows by now if he busts in he'll lose the bird. That also means chasing around until his tongue is dragging. He knows how to point, and he loves to do it. Just seeing the rod gets him excited. He has also learned to creep in by voice signal. Now, the object here is to set up the lesson in such a way that we will put the dog in a situation where he can follow the running bird, with caution. As in most of these lessons, we are not actually teaching — we're developing these instincts. Remember, the motion of the wing across the ground must be slow and smooth.

141. . . . He'll point in the craziest position. Start moving the bird across his path . . .

139. "He's not there, Beau, let's try to find him." Of course this is by sight but . . .

140. . . . it teaches him to be cautious. "You have him located. Now don't bolt" . . .

142. . . . Keep moving bird wing. Command WHOA to hold him. He'll sight follow . . .

143. . . . Command GO IN EEEZY. He starts to move to cut off bird. It develops instinct.

DANCING THE FLY ROD STALK

A fast-moving dog will force a running bird to take to the air. A dog has to learn that once he is on the trail of a bird, he has to move with caution. The command here is the EEEZY, GO IN. Draw out the EEE's in that command, it will force you to say it quietly. Try to keep the dog from getting too excited. The scent will be mighty overpowering to him. If he does break, WHOA him. Start him over again with the GO IN command.

This sequence exhibits the necessary restraint. Now he's under good control. He's associating command GO IN EEEZY with moving slowly. Stalk around obstacles.

Chapter 10

Fetch — An Essential Hunting Job

The Department of Interior's Fish and Wild Life Service can quote statistics as long as your arm giving chapter and verse on why a hunter should have a retrieving dog in the field. But, more powerful than all the statistics in the book is one unfortunate experience in the field. There is nothing more discouraging than a perfect point, a sensational shot, a dropped bird, and then — a lost bird. There is just no need to harp on this subject. Who would disagree? A dog is invaluable to ferret out crippled game. But, since you're a one-dog hunter, your dog must also double as a retriever. How do we go about teaching FETCH to an upland dog?

A Retriever is bred to retrieve. He just naturally takes to it like a duck to water, and he'll do that too. Let's first make a definition so we know what we are talking about. A dog that can be called a retriever is one that does the job on command, not just when the mood strikes him. This is a controlled retrieving.

There are many methods of training dogs to retrieve. They can all be classified into two groups; the natural retrieve and the forced retrieve.

For dogs that have been specifically bred for retrieving, the natural method usually works fine. Just as we have used a basic training tool, fly rod and wing, to teach the upland bird dog his main function in the field, retriever trainers have also a basic tool — the retrieving dummy. The retriever trainer uses the canvas-covered dummy to develop the natural instinct of the dog. He'll swing the dummy around in his hand, jump around himself, make a lot of noise and get the dog all excited. Then, he'll throw the dummy a short distance and the dog will go after it and pick it up. The trainer will run off from the dog, clap his hands, and the dog will come to the trainer carrying the dummy.

The correct commands are interjected into the game, and the dog learns what is expected of him. This play-game, like the rod and wing for the bird dog, develops the natural instinct to retrieve.

But — the bird dog was bred to point, and retrieving is a by-product. In most cases he will retrieve only when the mood is on him. When the going gets rough, he'd rather forget the whole thing and start looking for more birds to point. It certainly won't hurt to go through this natural retrieve method with your young dog, but sooner or later you want to make your dog a sure-fire retriever. When you have all the other control commands learned, then start on the force-retrieve system.

A word of warning here; don't play tug-of-war with a puppy that's expected to become a hunting dog. There's no need to teach him to be hard-mouthed as a puppy and expect him to handle a game bird with kid gloves when he grows up.

There are two ways to approach the force retrieve. Both work on the principle that the process will be taught backwards. The difference between the two methods is the degree of force that is necessary. This you will determine as you go along. Start with the system of less force, and if you do not make any progress on the first step in a few days, go to the second method, requiring more force.

Teaching the command FETCH is where a lot of novice trainers get into trouble. The reason is simple, and keep it in mind. We're teaching a dog to do something against his will. He's going to be called on to do this job when you want, and that may not be when he wants. He may take to this begrudgingly and without enthusiasm at first. But, after he gets the idea, he'll love it. Remember that your final product here will be a dog that will retrieve anything at the drop of a hat, and he'll do it on the run.

That reminds me of a story of the man teaching his dog to retrieve. He throws out a stick. The dog doesn't get the idea. He throws out another stick. The man gets down on all fours, runs out, picks up the stick in his mouth, comes back to the dog, and drops it at his feet. The man says to the dog, "Get the idea?" The dog kind of nods, picks up the stick, throws it out again. "Stop the nonsense!" says the man.

TEACH FETCH BACKWARDS — GENTLE FORCE AT FIRST

Any stick will do. We first teach the dog to take the stick in his mouth on the command FETCH. Then we will make him go to the stick, take it by mouth and bring it back. We increase the distance as we go. The first step is the crucial one, open the mouth and take, on command FETCH.

151. Open the dog's mouth by pressing the lower lip against his teeth. Put stick in his mouth and command FETCH! This may take 100 tries before he'll take it without prying his mouth open.

152. When he has this, hold muzzle closed and command HOLD. He should learn command fast. Start from the beginning. Each time go over FETCH command; get this one firmly in his noggin.

153. Start from the beginning. Command HOLD but don't hold muzzle. Instead give hand signal for hold. Repeat . . .

154. . . . then hold the stick a foot or so in front of him; command FETCH. Make him reach out for stick. He'll go for it.

155. Drop stick on the ground a few feet in front of him. Point to it. Give command FETCH. When you give this command do it in a firm voice, mean business.

156. Throw the stick out, have the dog wait for command, point at stick. Command FETCH. Gradually increase distance.

157. Lift him off his feet with choke collar. Command FETCH. He has to open, his air is cut.

FORCE-RETRIEVE BY FORCE

If the opening of the mouth by hand won't work, and with many dogs it won't — force is needed. Send the family off to a movie and settle this business with the dog. Put a choke collar on him, command FETCH, tighten up on the neck. He has to open his mouth for air. Put the stick in his mouth. Immediately release the pressure of the choke collar. With your hand gently around his muzzle have him hold the stick in his mouth. Praise him, pat him. This all sounds horrible, but in two days of short lessons with this method, the dog will start to open his mouth when you put the collar on. If he falters after he has learned this, the sight of the choke collar is usually all the reminder needed.

158. If he won't fetch, attach leash on the choke collar, place the leash under your foot . . .

159. . . . Command FETCH and pull leash, force the dog to the stick pulling his head down.

LET'S FINISH THE JOB IN STYLE

In a week of short lessons you are going to be over the rough stuff in the force retrieve. Throughout these lessons use your head. Keep changing your pace. Be firm when the situation calls for it, give him plenty of affection when he does something good, even if you've had to force him to do it. This is when a dog will try you to see if you're soft. If he sees that you give in when he puts the pressure on you by the hurt act, he'll never do the job with enthusiasm. But, gradually you'll see that his desire to please will win him over, and he'll bound out for the stick. Soon he will have so much fun at this, that he'll sit and demand encores. Throw the stick into your wife's shrubbery when both she and the dog aren't looking. Then command FETCH. Tell him to hunt it up. This he'll dig with relish.

When this all becomes a fun game, get him used to the idea of following your hand direction signal. Have him SIT, STAY before you send him off to retrieve. Then put your hand in front of his nose, command FETCH, and point with the hand and arm the direction in which the stick was thrown. Having him SIT, STAY will not be required in the field, but in the yard training it will teach him to depend on you, and later on in the field, if he's off direction on a downed bird, a hand signal can put him straight.

160. Once he gets the hang of this he loves it. Play the game with him often. Have him SIT, STAY. Throw out stick. When you give the command FETCH and he starts towards the stick keep repeating the command, FETCH, FETCH. Firmly repeating will keep him on the job. Later on if he doesn't see the object he'll hunt it up hearing the insistent, repeated voice command.

162. Firmly command HOLD. Give the definite signal. He'll soon enjoy this. But ...

163. ... do not let him decide when to drop the object. That's your job. Keep showing him hand signal.

HOLD — SOME DAY YOU'LL BRING HOME THE BACON

We haven't shown any pictures or discussed how you teach him to bring the stick to you. He has already learned COME. Use the same technique. When he picks up the stick, turn and run away from him. Clap your hands, call him, he'll bound for you. If he drops the stick, firmly command FETCH. Then command HOLD. Start to run from him, cheerfully calling him. When he reaches you, command firmly HOLD.

DROP — THIS IS THE END OF THE LINE

Don't pull a bird out of a dog's mouth. You know he has worked hard for it, and it is not his instinct to give it to you. Teaching him to DROP is the final touch of your long training process. He'll learn on the first bird he brings in that this whole game is played for you. Giving up the bird should teach him that. If you get in the habit of taking the bird from the dog's mouth, he may get in the habit of taking a firm hold on it to make it difficult for you. He could learn to get a hard mouth this way, and damage the game. Teaching to drop by flicking your finger on the end of his nose prevents this.

164. Command DROP, repeat it and flick him on the end of nose with the middle finger as you say . . .

165. . . . DROP, DROP. He'll not like this slap. He'll soon obey this when he sees finger.

There is no better place to continue the FETCH lessons than right in your own living room. At odd moments when the dog comes to you for attention you can keep practicing a few of the commands and make school more like a series of games. This is mentioned at this point because you have seen by the last few lessons that there is a good bit of pressure put on the dog in school. There are some hand-me-down ideas about training that should be put straight.

Living in a house in no way ruins the hunting instincts of a dog. Of course it is good to have a kennel run for the dog so that he can be out during the day. But, a dog that lives alone in a kennel doesn't have the opportunity to receive the love and affection that he needs and wants so badly. You are putting pressure on the dog during training. His reward is a friendly response from you. Make him a member of the family and your training will go easier. A dog sitting out in a lonely kennel can't develop the rapport with you that he can have living in your house.

I hunted quail last winter with a farmer in North Carolina. When we left his house to go by car to the first patch of cover, all the dogs, including mine, were put in the trunk of his new Chevrolet. The lid was

166. It only takes a minute of your time to keep him sharp to commands, happy.

closed and off we drove. He must have noticed the doubting expression on my face, because for the first five miles he told me that a hunting dog should not be allowed in a car . . . it ruins his nose. The smells of the inside of the car, the heater, tobacco, and so forth, desensitize a dog's nose. I asked him if his wife didn't think it cruel to jam the dogs in the trunk with the lid down, and he replied, "Hell, no! She won't let them in the car, they mess it up too much!" We drove the rest of the way to the cover in silence. I could see his cogs working. This little gem of hunting dog advice had nothing to do with the dog's nose — it was purely self-preservation for the farmer.

I have heard the same excuses about dogs living in kennels, and a little questioning usually reveals the real reason — they dirty up the rugs.

You're going to be working with your dog only a few minutes a day. Once he graduates from school, weeks might go by without any training. Of course this is good. Once a dog has learned his lessons you will only bore him by too much yard training. But running through these lessons for only a minute or two in the house will keep him sharp. It will satisfy the dog's need for attention, save time, and make your job easier.

167. Fetching a scrub brush will teach him to have soft mouth, hold a bird gently.

168. This is what we are going to end up with and don't think he does not love doing this.

THE ALL-PURPOSE DOG WILL FETCH IN WATER

A dog that lives near water will be in and out of it like a duck. A dog does not have to learn to swim, he just swims. But, the problem with a dog that has no occasion to swim on his own, is that he sees no need to act like a fish. This is especially true with the upland game breeds, which have not been bred for the job.

This dog, your one-and-all-purpose dog, has to learn to FETCH in water. We're not doing this to make a waterfowl dog of him. But in the winter, you'll be able to send your upland dog into cold water to retrieve a bird downed over water. Of course he has to continue to hunt after the retrieve to get warm. The coats of retrievers protect them from the frigid water. They can come back from a cold swim, sit in a cold blind, and still be warm. The main purpose of this training is to save for the table the occasional bird that you drop in water.

We ran a very interesting experiment with Beau. The whole thing was documented with the camera. Now remember, we don't have to teach a dog to swim, we only have to teach him to like to do it. We went through the whole conventional method of getting him to swim and FETCH in the water. Then we taught him with the rod and wing.

I went into the water, I coaxed, cajoled, begged, clapped my hands, called his name, blew the whistle, and did everything I could think of to make him come in and swim. Oh, how he wanted to get to me. He ran up and down the bank looking for a way to reach me. He waded out as far as he dared, but could not get the nerve to make the plunge. I just could not make him do it by himself.

I finally had to resort to using the leash. He has always had to do what was expected of him when the leash was on. The leash is a symbol of control to him. He did not like it, but this was the only alternative I had after a long time of coaxing. I attached the leash and very slowly walked him in, talking in a pleasant tone to him the whole time.

This didn't help the situation. He could not be coaxed back in again. Then we changed tactics. I threw out a stick and commanded FETCH. He would only do it if the leash was attached to the collar. I didn't have to hold the leash. He would drag it in, he knew that the leash meant control, and I could make him do it if I wanted to. Reluctantly he went in.

Finally he started to do it without the leash on voice command. But it took pressure. Commands had to be repeated. It was a sad performance. Although he obeyed, he hated this fish business.

THE ALL-PURPOSE DOG WILL FETCH IN WATER

169. I coaxed and tried hard to make him come. He wanted to, but couldn't get up nerve . . .

170. . . . Neither of us relished this technique. I put him on the leash which means control to him. I walked him slowly until he had to swim. Off he went, he only turned and headed straight back for the shore.

172. I showed him the stick. Threw it so . . . **173.** ...he only waded. I commanded FETCH...

174. . . . Then threw it into deeper water. Under duress he swam the few feet and . . .

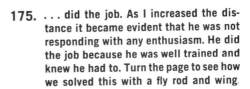

175. . . . did the job. As I increased the distance it became evident that he was not responding with any enthusiasm. He did the job because he was well trained and knew he had to. Turn the page to see how we solved this with a fly rod and wing.

THE ROD AND WING SAVES THE DAY

Beau has a fixation about the fly rod and wing. As you've seen before, he'll play with this till hell freezes over. We'll use the wing, it'll be the incentive. Before we used this technique we couldn't get him in the water, except under pressure. Now, we can't keep him out of the water. He dives in with enthusiasm.

176. I showed him the fly rod and the wing. He's anxious. I flipped it over the . . .

177. . . . water. The very first time, he dove in. From then on it was like duck soup.

178. Now he had an incentive. He swam after the bird wing just as long as my arm held out.

179. We had it made. Overnight, the wing gave this a meaning for him. He loved to dive.

LET'S PLAY LIKE A LABRADOR RETRIEVER

Take the wing off the rod, tie it to a stick. Now he will fetch with enthusiasm as long as your arm will last. He has changed his attitude about this in a matter of minutes. I can't take him in a boat any more when I go fishing. The rod gets him excited, and on the first cast he is overboard swimming after the dry fly.

180. This is the first step in the transfer from the rod and wing to retrieving of game . . .

181. ...The throw...

182. ...The fetch...

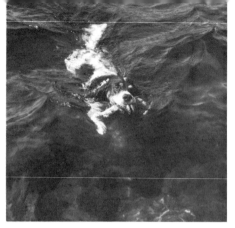

183. . . . The last step of this game is easy. A bird was released over the water and shot. The FETCH command was given. Out he plunged, he retrieved in style. No problem now.

Chapter 11

The Gun

There is always much discussion on the subject of gun-shyness and the hunting puppy. It's greatly exaggerated. Gun-shyness in trained hunting dogs is rare, and most of the cases one hears about involve dogs that have not been trained. They occasionally go into the field to hunt, but they don't know what it's all about and neither does the hunter. A good loud blast of a 12-gauge gun in the ear of one of these dogs who has been living on social security will, of course, naturally scare the hell out of him.

There is no need to get into a debate about the effect of a gun on a dog. This problem is so easy to prevent with proper training, that it's only good insurance to go ahead with this preventive medicine.

Conditioning, repeated conditioning, is the answer to much of the training of a dog. Unconsciously he will learn that a loud report is associated with something good, and he won't fear it. Back in the pre-school chapter, we discussed the four aspects of early learning. The third aspect was putting up with irritations. This is another of the irritations he gets. At this tender age we start the preparation for the gun.

At mealtime, which is certainly one of the most pleasant times in a puppy's day, we will shoot off a cap pistol. He will associate this irritation, the noise, with something good, the food, and learn to put up with it. This in itself will solve the problem, because the dog is so very flexible at this age.

186. During preschool, shoot the cap pistol off while he eats. The irritation at this time teaches him two things: to put up with some discomfort, and that a loud noise is not going to hurt him. In fact the noise means something good — food.

187. Since the noise didn't hurt him at mealtime, let's show him under conditions close to those he will see when he hunts. Command GO IN EEEZY. Then WHOA him. Walk ahead of him, have him hold and you flush the bird. Shoot off the gun. If we wanted, this is where we would teach the dog drop or steady-to-wing-and-shot. It's discussed later.

BACK TO THE ROD AND WING

At mealtime we have been conditioning him to the bang. But, he has not known why you have been doing this. He has just accepted it as one of the master's queer ways.

Now, we're ready to give him some idea of what that loud noise is for and when he will hear it. Here is where he gets conditioned for the shotgun in the field. In the rod and wing chapter, when we taught command GO IN — EEEZY, we also taught him to hold point while you, the hunter, moved in ahead to flush the bird. We will now introduce the gun as we move in to flush the game. Pick up the feather, fly it, and shoot off the gun. Pointing, like eating, is something else he likes to do. So, the noise again is associated with something good. From now on you should stop shooting off the cap pistol at mealtime. At this time, let him associate the bang of a gun with the point. Then, when it happens in the field it won't be unexpected.

NOW FOR THE REAL GUN

There is usually much difference of opinion as to when the gun should be introduced. Using this system, the time is determined by when you reach this point in the rod and wing training. You'll need the cooperation of a few friends plus your wife, if you have one.

Go out to a field and set up a hand trap. Have everybody shoot in rotation. Have them start to fire away when you're approximately two hundred yards away with the dog on a leash. Start to walk the dog toward them. Stop and talk gently to him. Note his reaction to the noise. I'll bet 100 to 1 that he will pull to get up to the firing line. Have the person he knows best on the firing line, your wife perhaps, walk down to meet you. Let him see that if she was up there it can't be so bad. Both of you slowly walk the dog closer to the firing. Stop and have her go back and fire at a few birds. Then, have her come back and you go up and fire. I'm sure the dog will then lead her up to you. He'll see the clay birds fly, get all excited, and want to go out and retrieve them for you.

Now, this should satisfy you. Your dog's been prepared for this, he's been bred for this. There is no need for you to worry any further. The whole lesson has been for you. The dog learned all this in preschool.

188. On a leash, 200 yards from the firing...   **189.** ... walk him up slowly. Talk softly...

190. . . . Someone from firing line come . . .

191. . . . play with him, reassure him. Then . . .

192. . . . both walk him closer. Back off if . . .

193. . . . noise bothers him, but it won't . . .

194. . . . Your wife then goes up to shoot . . .   **195.** . . . When you go he'll want to retrieve.

Chapter 12

A Little Courtesy, Please —
Honor the Other Dog's Point

Backing or honoring is one of the essentials and also one of the beautiful aspects of hunting with well-trained dogs. There's nothing more exciting than dogs working as a team. I have a serious word of warning here. Nothing can help your dog more than working in the field with other well-trained dogs. At the same time, nothing can do your dog more harm than being in the field with an uncontrolled dog. This is a very touchy business, for as the old saying goes, "You can criticize a man's wife, but don't you say one word about his dog." Well, maybe you can't say anything about it, but you sure can do something about it. Don't hunt your dogs together.

That doesn't mean that you can't go on a hunting trip with a cronie who can't handle his dog. Put your dog down for a time, and then his dog, or hunt separate covers. But, in a nice way, let it be known that if he wants to hunt the dogs together he's going to have to put in some overtime homework before you'll agree.

Here's the kind of trouble that you are asking for, if you don't heed this advice.

If the other fellow's dog pays no mind to his whistle and he's blowing it all day, this is going to confuse your dog. If your dog's working in range, but a whistle keeps blasting away to bring the other dog back, your dog won't be hunting — he'll be checking — to see if it's you blowing your head off.

Now, dogs are very jealous critters when it comes to game. You can see this when a couple of dogs are racing for a retrieve. They will go all out to get there first. This will help a slow retriever. He will soon learn to stop the pottering around and get busy and get the bird. But, the same jealousy applies to the finding of the game and to the point. It's going to upset your dog if he sees the uncontrolled dog bumping up birds way out ahead, when he knows that he's not allowed to roam way out. Needless to say, this will also upset other members of the hunting party.

But, the cardinal sin is the dog that busts in ahead of a dog on point. The first dog on point may break and rush in to protect his interest and flush the bird. I have seen some canine old-timers abandon point and give the inconsiderate young fool the licking of his life. I heard of one situation where a dog was on point and another dog busted in on him and flushed the bird. The owner of the dog on point put down his gun and busted one on the nose of the owner of the disrespectful critter saying, "If a dog's selfish, it's because his boss is selfish, and I hate inconsiderate, selfish people."

How do you keep from getting a bust in the nose? Teach your dog to back or honor another dog's point. Start off with the rod and wing game. You need two dogs. Put one on point. When the other is brought into the yard he should be WHOAED as soon as he sees the first dog on point. Hold the backing dog on point. Repeat this until the second dog stops without command when he sees the first dog on point.

Just to show how easy this is, the ten-week-old puppy was put on point. I called for Beau, who was not in the yard, and gave the command WHOA.

196. Beau was taught to back the pup. The pup was put on point, then Beau was told WHOA.

197. Just for fun, to show how easy this is, we reversed the honor and had the puppy back Beau. This ten-week pup was trained for all the pictures in the book in one weekend.

The rod and wing will save the one-dog hunter a lot of time here. If two dogs are hunting together continuously they will have many opportunities to learn this lesson. But, in just a few sessions, you and a friend can teach this to your dogs before the bird season opens. Honoring is sight pointing, not pointing on scent. When he sees a dog on point, he stops and points too. The rod and wing teaches this directly, no transfer to the field is needed.

The conventional method of teaching this in the field is to WHOA the dog that is learning to back as soon as the first dog goes on point. Then go to your dog. Lead him up to a place where he can see the pointing dog, then WHOA him again. Hold him on point; gently stroke him until the bird is flushed and shot. If he still does not get the idea when you first WHOA him, put him on a leash, lead him in behind the pointing dog until he gets the scent. Then he'll point. Pick him up bodily and move him a yard or so to the rear. Set him down to point again behind the lead dog.

HONOR THE OTHER DOG'S POINT

198. Backing is so easy to transfer under field conditions if it is learned in the yard ...

199. ... It's done on sight not scent in the field. Bring in second dog, WHOA him when he ...

200. ... sees the first dog on point. If he falters, take him out of the yard, start over.

201. When the first dog goes on point bring the dog learning to honor up on lead . . .

202. . . . just behind the dog that is holding set him on point. Softly WHOA him . . .

203. . . . Let him get the scent. WHOA him, don't let him move ahead of pointer . . .

126

204. ... Pick him up, he may stay on point in your arms. This won't disturb him...

205. ... Set him down a few yards behind pointing dog, stroke him. He learns...

206. ... that he is not to move up on other dog, so he does next best—the stretch.

207. This is the way it works on quail.

208. Dan Norman's dogs honor Beau's point. Did you ever see such a beautiful sight?

STEADY-TO-WING-AND-SHOT — A COURTESY TO THE HUNTER

Many an evening has been wasted arguing whether a gun dog should be taught steady-to-wing-and-shot, or drop-to-flush-and-wing. Let me kiss off drop-to-flush-and-wing fast. We have shown you that your gun dog's going to have to be a sure-fire retriever. He can't mark down a bird, he won't see it, if he's lying on his belly when you shoot. As far as this one goes — forget it.

For the field trial dog, steady-to-wing-and-shot is a must. It's just part of the rules of the game, it looks stylish. But, this is a gun dog, not a field trialer we're training, so let's look at this from the standpoint of the average guy hunting for the table.

A dog that chases a low-flying flushed bird is in danger of being shot by a careless gun handler; or, if the gunners had enough good sense to hold their fire it could mean a lost bird. This is good reason for teaching steadiness to your dog. Although, a word of caution to the hunting party about a retrieving dog that breaks at flush, will prevent such an accident. We have a rule, if a man hollers "Hold fire!" we hold fire, and no questions asked.

A dog that holds to wing-and-shot won't inadvertently flush a sleeper before the guns can be reloaded. It could mean another lost bird, if he races to get downed game. But, I've seen the dog on the retrieve to a downed bird throw on the brakes and jam on point. His point looked more as though he slammed into a stone wall. Also, it's not uncommon to see a dog return from a retrieve with bird in mouth, stop, and go up on point. Unfortunately, any time this has happened I've been carrying a loaded double instead of a loaded camera.

I feel, as you can see, that it's more important a dog be stanch on point. Forget about this finishing touch, an affected mannerism, merely a courtesy a dog shows a hunter. A fast retriever, over the years, will save more game than the occasional sleeper lost. Trainers will agree it's easier to teach steadiness to a dog that is not trained to retrieve. The sight of falling game is a powerful temptation to the dog that loves to retrieve. Weighing all the facts, I don't want to impede this all important function — to fetch.

I hunted with a fellow who trained his dog to point, hold, then after the kill, point dead birds instead of retrieving. He dropped a quail in a thick briar patch. The dog held point beautifully as the man, on all fours, climbed in for the bird. He came out a bloody mess; next time it happened his dog pointed as I sent my dog in for the bird.

Steadiness is just one more thing you would have to teach a dog that is contrary to his natural instinct. I don't think it's worth it, but if you insist on this one, the rod and wing will save you much time. I didn't list it as the thirteenth job of the rod and wing; it wasn't because I'm superstitious, it's because I'm practical.

When you move in ahead of the dog on point (See picture 187), fly the wing, shoot off the gun. Command WHOA. He will associate the bang and the flying feather with the command WHOA. Once he has this, reverse the order. Command WHOA, then fly the wing and shoot. By the time you are ready to teach this rod and wing lesson a dog will be under such good control he'll learn this in one lesson. Teaching this on live birds in the field presents a lot of problems. You'll need an assistant to flush the birds while you handle the dog on a check cord. As he breaks for the bird on flush, send him spinning. Take him back to the place he pointed and hold him in the point position and bellow WHOA. Repeat and repeat all this until the dog responds.

The best advice is never to let a dog break on flush, never let him get the habit. Of course, don't *you* be an eager beaver. If you bust in all excited for a downed bird, your dog will do the same. If you're to teach your dog steadiness, show a little yourself. If he does get the taste of the chase, you're going to have a hell of a time changing his mind about this one. Field trainers advise this no-breaking rule, yet at the same time they advise the trainer to let a young dog break to whet his appetite for hunting. Trial judges will mark a dog down if he appears to be too mechanical, yet they insist on steadiness to wing and shot which in my estimation is just not for the amateur trainer.

Let the dog retrieve — you'll eat better.

Chapter 13

The Game Is For the Birds

The increase in the number of hunters and the decrease in amount of game and hunting land has made it economically feasible to have hunting preserves in almost every locale in the U.S. This is pay-as-you-go shooting. Many old-timers claim it's like shooting fish in a barrel. That can be true, but it can also be some of the toughest hunting you'd want.

At a good preserve, the proprietor can set it up any way you want it. I've hunted with skeptics on preserves, I've seen them come in at sundown, wipe their brow, suck on a can of beer, and admit it was a good, tough hunt.

But our job here is not to sell preserves, it's to train dogs. During the open season, it's great sport to hunt open land, and it costs only the price of a license, but these seasons are so short that it's really to our advantage to have the game preserves. On preserves we can run our dogs six months a year and, in some states, all year round.

During the open season I'll take grouse, woodcock, and quail as my meat. There is no better bird than the woodcock to train a young dog on. However, this is strictly a regional problem. In the Midwest where pheasant is abundant, that's the bird for the upland hunter. Mr. Pheasant is a tricky bird. He'd rather run than fly, so he can play hell with a young dog. In the East the pheasant season is so short that it makes little sense to train the dog on this crafty, fleet-footed fellow. Your problems will be fewer if you use quail. The quail acts more like the grouse and the woodcock which can only be found in the wild.

Pigeons can be used. They're inexpensive, easily available, and can be used off season. They give a good scent and are strong flyers.

Another fine bird for training purposes is the Japanese quail or the coturnix. All you do is take eight or ten birds in a box, walk through cover that has open trees, and like a farmer sowing seed, drop the birds at random.

They'll crawl into the brush, give off a strong scent, and hold exceedingly well for the dogs. The cover must have open trees so the birds will tower when they fly, otherwise they will skim along the ground. In the right cover, they make sporty shooting.

The only reason this bird hasn't become popular is that he can't be stocked. Overnight he's gone. Much money has been spent to find out where he goes, but the best biologists haven't yet found the answer. My guess is back to Japan.

This will give you some idea of the game birds that are available, but since this is actually a regional issue, better ask a few questions around and see what the other fellows are using.

Whatever bird you use, there's one problem that you should be aware of. Some dogs have an uncanny ability to track down a man by scent, and they have good enough noses to get man-scent on planted birds. I saw this demonstrated, beyond doubt.

A trainer took two quail. The first one he planted in thick cover two hundred yards from where the dog would start to hunt. The dog didn't see him plant the bird. The dog was cast off to hunt. On the second cast he picked up the man's scent, followed it directly to the bird, and lay down next to it. In other words, the man-scent threw the dog off completely, thereby disrupting his entire hunting sequence. He didn't make game, he didn't point. When he found the bird he just lay down and waited. The second bird was released by letting it fly off the hand of the trainer. The dog didn't see it fly for one hundred yards or so, then settle into the cover. Again the dog was cast off. This time he had to hunt. The trainer brought him toward the bird from downwind. When this young setter got the scent he jammed into one of the prettiest points you ever saw. What did this prove? To get the best out of a dog and a bird, the bird has to be air washed by flight after it has been handled by man.

BIRD RELEASING DEVICES

There are quite a few bird releasing devices on the market. In one form or the other, they are great big rattraps in reverse. They hold the bird, then throw it in the air at the propitious moment. The best one I have used is made by Jack Stuart, a damn fine dog trainer, in Farwell, Michigan. He makes three models. They'll toss a pheasant or a few quail ten feet in the air, and what's more, one model does it by pulling a string, another by pushing a button on a twenty-five-foot cord, and the third will do it by radio from a few hundred yards away. There's only one problem with all these things — I'd rather go bird hunting than make like a mechanical engineer.

There's another device, and I don't like it either, but I guess I should mention it because lots of folks use it; but then, lots of folks pick fights with drunks, too, and I don't like that either. This is the rocked bird technique. You take a bird in your hands, put his head under his wing, swing him around over your head a few times, then you lay him in some cover on his side and he'll lie there like a sailor sleeping off a drunk. Then you bring your dog in to hunt. It will serve you right if the dog picks up man scent and lays down next to the bird looking up at you with the "what-should-I-do-now-Boss?" expression. The real answer to the trainer's needs is the quail box. Is it a device? Maybe so, but we're just helping the Mother Nature out a bit. It's this simple:

Nature has made the quail in such a way that he lives in a family or coveys. During the day when the family is hungry they go out in a field and eat. But they don't roam off too far from one another. Then, when they feel sociable again they whistle each other back home. They're smarter than man, though. When he has a meeting of his whole clan they sit around facing each other, which usually leads to fights. The quail sit around a circle too, but with the talking end facing outward.

Actually, we don't care which way he faces, the thing that interests us is that he whistles himself, and all the rest of the clan back home. All we have to do is make a home for him to live in. We're going to furnish each family with a rent-free apartment. We now put the quail on social security, feed and water him the days we don't use him. This apartment house has to have two apartments, one for each family. They can be any size, depending on the number of birds you want in each family.

Carry this house to the center of a field. Leave it there for a few days. Let the birds get acclimated to their surroundings. Then open the door of one of the apartments, and flush the birds out. They will scatter all over the field. Give them time to move around looking for food or cover, then they will have left scent for the dogs. Bring the dog into the field from downwind and start the hunt. You can decide ahead of time how many of the birds you are going to kill, because those you don't kill will be saved for the next day. Here's how that works: Meanwhile back at the ranch, the quail living in the second apartment are still there. Feeling neglected, they will start to call the other family back. All the birds that have survived your rather sad exhibition with the shotgun will covey up back in their apartment. The next time you wish to give your dog a workout or improve your shooting, flush the family that lived in the second apartment, then let the first family call them back.

The quail box can be made any size, and this is a real advantage. If you don't have an old chicken coop on your property that can be turned

Quail Call Box

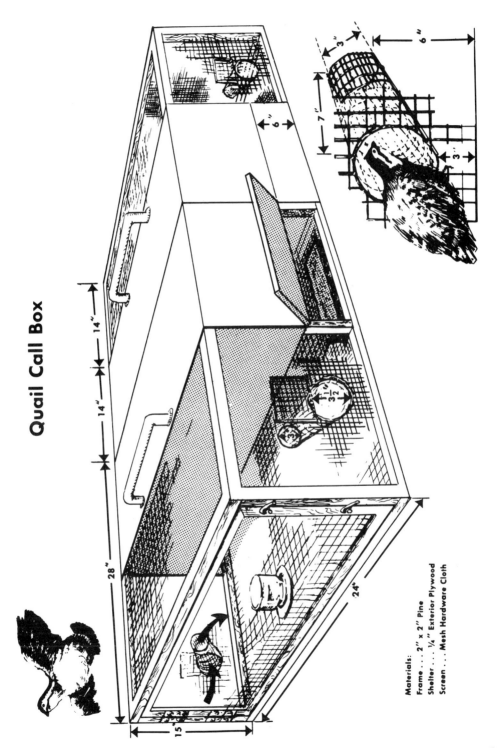

Materials:
Frame . . . . 2″ x 2″ Pine
Shelter . . . . ¼″ Exterior Plywood
Screen . . . . Mesh Hardware Cloth

135

into a big quail box, make a portable one that can be kept in your garage, and transport it in your car to the field. Make a business deal with a farmer to use his land. You only need twenty or thirty acres. Maybe for a few bucks the farmer's boy will carry the box back in the barn at night, feed and water the birds all week for you. In this way, you won't have to stay around the few hours it takes for all the birds to be called back home.

Check with your local game warden or your state conservation department. You may need a license to operate with live birds. Since this is dog training and not a commercial venture, the license is usually only a couple of bucks.

There are many designs for the quail box. One calls for a big cage for the birds that are going to be flushed, and a small cage for a few quail that will always remain and act as the callers. I don't care for this design. As novice bird raisers, we won't know which are the strong callers, and the few birds we put in the small cage may not call the flushed birds home. I like to have the birds evenly divided. This is just a matter of insurance. Then alternate the flights of the two coveys.

Build the two attached cages out of hardware cloth. Start by making a wooden frame which should include a plywood shelter. Build in water jars and feed troughs. One side of each cage swings open on hinges to allow the birds to escape. After that covey is flushed, the door is closed. The other covey acts as callers. On two sides of the cage entrance ways are made for the birds to return. They are placed three inches off the ground, the height of the bird's eye as he walks. He'll then see it on returning to the cage. On the inside of these portholes we will attach seven-inch cones made of the wire hardware cloth. The quail will jump up into the porthole, walk through the narrowing tunnel of the cone, and drop off into the cage. These cones narrow down from three and a half inches in diameter to three. When they are attached to the portholes, they should be given an upward tilt. The smaller end of the cone, which is inside the box, will then be above the quail's head and he won't know how to get out. On the outside of the cage, a flap of wire cloth should be attached next to the cones to act as a door. When the birds are all in, the entrance cones are closed; when the birds come back to the box they will go into the correct cage; also, predators can't get at the birds.

211. This is what the quail box looks like. Set it out ahead of time. Get birds used to it.

212. The quail who naturally live in coveys learn to go up the ramp to get back home safely.

Chapter 14

Now to Reap the Harvest

It seems to have taken us a long time to get here, but, your puppy could be as young as five months old. Following the system we have laid out, the date you put him on his first birds depends primarily on when the dog was born and when the bird season opens, not the calendar years formerly recommended by traditional training methods. Your puppy is ready. Remember, we can't teach a dog *to* hunt, we can only teach him *how to* hunt. Breeding takes care of the first part, you and this accelerated training method take care of the second.

If you have not worried about it yourself, someone is sure to bring up, with a touch of envy in his voice, the question of a *mechanical dog*. Naturally this dog will be mechanical in the field the first few times. He may rely on you for directions. He'll check on you often; after all, the two of you have worked very closely, you're like father and mother to him. Being young and inexperienced with a strong desire to please you, he'll be a little unsure of himself, wanting to be sure to do what you want. *Don't worry about it!* He's basically a hunting dog and will grow more independent; he'll gain security and do an adult job when he is an adult.

He'll quickly recognize the purpose of all this training, and find the proper role in the team of gun and dog. But, even his first trip to the field will be successful, he'll be under fine control, and you will be able to start transferring all he has learned in the yard to the field. Very soon the sight of a gun means game and everything the dog lives for comes into being.

The first few times you take your dog out, you'll be taking *him* hunting; after that he'll be taking *you*. He'll know where the birds are before you will. Give him his head. Get out and hunt the dog. Put him on birds, this is where the dog is really made. We've given him preflight training, now it's time for him to solo. And I mean solo. Don't hunt with other dogs for a while, get him firmly on the job first.

From time to time your dog will make mistakes, and so will you. Go back over the commands in the yard. After all, if you kill 60 per cent of the birds your dog points you're doing damn well. Take this into consideration when he makes a mistake. A round of skeet every once in a while is your yard training to work out your mistakes.

Some days there're going to be plenty of things that your dog will do to make you mad and him glad: busting birds, chasing rabbits, false pointing, not obeying WHOA instantly, and even being too interested in hunting to pay attention to you. And, remember, the finest dog in the world will sometimes pass by a bird.

But, when you have to reprimand the dog you can be sure he knows why — he knows what the commands mean from the training. There's nothing in the field training that takes precedence over the fact that the dog is not to be reprimanded unless he knows he has done wrong. Otherwise you are going to confuse him. That's why we have spent so much time teaching the commands with the rod and wing. They prepare him for field training and teach the necessary vocabulary for field work. Now this vocabulary has to be transferred into action on game. This whole fly rod training negates the possibility of blind punishment. Blind punishment is punishment the dog receives without his being sure of the reason. This kind of reprimand can take more of the hunting zip out of your dog than any other single thing. A popular misconception is that curbing a dog's range lessens his initiative. This I refute — but, blind punishment *will* take the zip out of him.

WATCH YOUR DOG FOR SIGNS OF TIRING

We have done a lot of talking about the mental development of your dog. Let's look at the physical aspects of his growth. I believe here that the 1 to 7 ratio is a good indicator. A three-year-old dog is like a twenty-one-year-old man — both are in their prime. A six-month-old puppy is like a three-and-a-half-year-old child. Just ask any mother how much energy a child of that age has. They can wear out a grown woman. Enough said. But, don't run a young puppy too hard, don't overtire him. Make him love hunting not dread being knocked out. Give him plenty of rest periods during the workout and plenty of time between hunts.

STOP ON A DIME IN THE FIELD

WHOA. . . . Did you stop reading? Good, now you're thinking like a dog. This command, as you know, is the most important vocal command in the dog's repertoire.

WHOA was first taught as a violent hand signal in the yard, then with the fly rod. By this time, when you take him into the field, he'll have a good understanding of the command. Remember though, for most young dogs the game smells are too much — they almost go berserk with excitement. The dog's basic instinct here is to rush in and grab the bird. Of course, many dogs will point their first bird, but if they don't, in these early hunting experiences, there are two ways of handling this situation.

If the pup pays no heed to the command WHOA and flushes or bumps the bird, do not shoot the bird. Teach the dog no WHOA, no bird. The dog will chase off after the bird. Still excited, he'll rush back to the source of those wonderful smells. Grab him when he is making game at the spot from where the bird flushed. Hold him roughly by the scruff of the neck and by the skin over the rump in the point position. Bellow at him . . . WHOA . . . WHOA . . . WHOA. A few of these and he'll get the idea. The dog can't blame you if the bird is lost.

213. If he bumps bird, runs back for those intoxicating smells, teach him no WHOA, no bird.

Now maybe you see why it's so very important to have the dog working close to you. You're not going to be able to do a damn thing in this situation if you don't see what has happened and be able to be close by to make corrections, *immediately*. This is the reason I have reversed the range pattern that the dog has traditionally been taught.

The second method is the check cord, to be used only if the first fails.

The dog drags a fifty-foot nylon rope attached to his collar. It helps to slow up a dog that is too vigorous in the field. The idea here is for you to get hold of the cord in time to give the WHOA command. If he does not stop, *yank*. Spill him head over heels.

214. WHOA or learn the ropes. Disobey? Yank! Spill him head over heels with the check cord.

I do not care too much for this. I can never seem to get the rope in time. But, more important, I don't like what it does to a dog. If you were just about to eat a piece of chocolate cake and at the precise moment when you were putting it in your mouth you were flattened, you might soon learn to dislike cake. Also, a smart dog gets rope-wise. He will WHOA only on the rope, or he may decide not to hunt with the rope on. A word of warning here. If you have to use this system because your dog is headstrong, wear gloves. Nylon rope (which is good because it will slip around brush) can give a terrible rope burn. Don't give up on the first method too soon.

215. The cord is almost impossible to reach him when you want, then when you do—tangled.

You may have to resort to this method if you train on birds like pheasant, that run. Many times a young dog will jam up on a fine point, then see the bird run off. This is just too much for him, and off he goes. The check cord, of course, will stop him. Then you can get to him and give the GO IN EEEZY command. He will then learn that you don't want him to chase, but want him to stalk. Gosh, but the pheasant is a nasty critter, except on the table!

Another warning! Inexperienced trainers, knowing how important the WHOA command is, have a temptation to be too harsh on the early experiences the dog has when transferring the WHOA command from rod and wing in the yard to birds in the field. If the dog seems to be confused, not bull-headed about rushing in, but *confused,* slow up on this command.

A dog that takes his mind off the bird on a loud, harsh WHOA command, is confused. He may back off. He may lie down or turn and look at you. If this rather rare problem happens, it's because you're too excited.

Soften up on the command. Remove the excitement from your voice. True, this is the peak or climax of the sport for both of you. If you stay under control he'll learn what is expected of him. If you're too anxious for meat, buy it from the butcher. It'll be cheaper and less frustrating.

Don't be afraid while teaching WHOA to let the young dog bust a few birds. It will develop his enthusiasm to hunt.

CHASING FUR

Every young dog will chase or point rabbits, stink birds, butterflies, or anything else, including things dead. It's nothing to worry about. The scent of game birds will take over eventually when he comes to realize that's what you're after.

If he chases songbirds, whistle him in. If he obeys the whistle, of course don't reprimand him for chasing the birds. If he doesn't obey, the punishment is then for two things he's done wrong. Continually calling him off the stink birds will give him the idea that you're not interested in them.

If he chases fur, get to him, command repeatedly a stern NO, NO. Take off your hat and make a threatening gesture with it as if you are going to spank him. He'll lie down, get very close to him, bellow repeatedly NO. Go to strike him again. Change the tone of your voice and send him on to hunt.

216. When he does something wrong, chasing rabbits or song birds, command NO. Make firm.

COMMUNICATIONS

To be successful in the field with your dog, you're going to have to be a specialist in communications. All communications are two-way streets and your dog has many outward manifestations of practically talking to you. Most of the training has dealt with what you have to say to the dog. In the field you must learn to know what he tells you and to anticipate him. Of course his means of telling you will be in the form of pantomime. For example:

When he comes across a cold trail scent he makes it known by a wag of the tail. If the trail gets hot his tail movements will be sharper and his whole being will become more intensely animated. He'll give a new expression when he is hot on the birds and still another when the birds are found. If in doubt at any point he may stop and give a stance that is easily distinguished from a true point.

A hunter who understands the dog's pantomime saves himself headaches and greatly adds to his pleasure of working with a dog. The dog will be trained faster because the trainer will anticipate the dog and avoid any rash actions. Dogs are much more given to studying the expressions of the handler than is generally supposed. Men can say to a man one thing and mean another, but a dog doesn't have that facility. He depends on actions and expressions, so the handler must be consistent in the way he handles the dog in the field. For example, many times while the dog is quartering the field, he may glance back to keep you in sight. If you consistently pay no heed and just go on about your business of hunting, he'll read this as a signal and learn to do the same. You will then see if you change your tactics, stop and just look at your dog, he will come in to see what you want.

FALSE POINT

A dog that shows a tendency of being a false pointer can easily be broken of this habit if you know what's going on in his upstairs. Sending him on to hunt at the propitious moment will soon teach him that you want him to stop and point only the real thing — body scent. Sending him on is your way of ignoring what he is trying to say to you. It's like saying to a child, "I don't want to see you do that again."

There aren't many dogs that are false pointers. It's more apt to happen with a dog that works in a team of two dogs for one hunter. The false pointer in a brace may want attention, like a second child who raises hell, knowing it would bring a response from mother, whether good or bad.

Make sure in this false pointing business that something didn't happen that was beyond the dog's control. A dog will point fresh scent of a bird that flushed unseen, or he may be a very cautious dog. This is not his fault, and his nose tells him a bird is there. A real false pointer is a chronic offender.

POTTERING

Pottering, the stopping and sniffing of foot scents, is a fault common to young dogs and can be corrected easily when understood by the handler. When the dog gives the trainer this signal, the handler must signal back that that's not wanted. Move the dog on sternly. Remember though, a young dog knows little about the difference in scents. Sending him on will soon teach him that you're not interested in the meat on the feet — you want the breast.

But, be sure to tell him when he does point the birds that that's what you like. Get to the dog as soon as possible, without rushing in, gently stroke him, talk soothingly. He'll know what you mean.

If your dog insists on being a pottering slowpoke and has not learned from his own experience that with head high he can use the wind to advantage, or if he's a chronic false pointer, set up this situation. Release a few quail and mark them down well. Take the dog down wind, then cast him off. Work him very fast right into the birds. If he drops his head, urge him on faster. He'll most likely blunder into the bird and flush it. But, he'll soon learn that foot scents mean birds are near and he'll automatically show interest and race on, forgetting about faint scents.

Don't worry about his going too fast at this time. Always try to work your dog into the wind. A dog with a fair nose can go at a gallop and slam on the brakes in time, *if* his mind and nose are working ahead of him and not at his own feet. Teaching a dog this gives him confidence.

THE BOLTER

The bolter, or the self-hunter who hunts where he pleases, either was started too late in his training, or he was trained as a field trialer. The demands for pace and range in trialing develops this fault in dogs. Before the 1880's, bolting was not even heard of in a gun dog. When the ways of hunting to the gun were abandoned for field trials, the problem developed. You won't have that problem following this teaching system. From a puppy we have taught the dog to work *with* you, under control.

BLINKING

The blinker, a dog that leaves the point before you reach him, is another problem you won't have. I have heard it said that the sound of the rising bird or covey causes this. Nonsense. The dog is afraid of something. Either it's the sound of the gun, which early training prevents, or he was

145

too roughly handled and confused when taught steady-to-wing-and-shot. Since we don't recommend this practice, the blinking problem won't arise, unless you are too stern at first on the WHOA command in the field.

A dog can develop a habit that is similar to blinking, but not quite the same thing. If he is allowed to work too far ahead of the gun he may get tired on point and move off and come in on the birds from another direction. This can develop into a blinking habit. Your dog has been taught to work for the gun, so the time lapse won't occur.

MORE TIPS ON COMMUNICATIONS

Let's assume that you have trained the dog to work and retrieve quail. Then you go hunting and kill a woodcock over the dog. He may not retrieve. Don't force him to do it. Go retrieve the bird yourself and take the dog along. Sit down, fondle the bird and the dog. Show him that you like this thing that has a different smell and a different feel. Then throw the bird, put the dog through the FETCH, HOLD, DROP commands. Praise him and put the bird in your bag. There is no better way of explaining to him that this is what you want.

I won the easiest bet of my life the first time Beau was in a hunting party that dropped a woodcock. The bird was not shot over Beau, the hunter fetched the bird himself and came back to show it while we all stopped for a smoke. The subject got around to an old theory that some dogs won't fetch woodcock because of the taste. One word from me, "nonsense!" brought the challenge of a dollar bet.

I went through the play procedure with Beau and the bird, then threw the bird and commanded FETCH DEAD. Beau reached the bird, hesitated, and looked at me. The command was given again and he fetched. Three times that day Beau fetched downed woodcock without command. My dollarless friend just scratched his head. It cost him to learn that a dog force-trained to retrieve will bring back anything you want if he can carry it.

In the field, add the word DEAD to the FETCH command.

After the dog is trained you will find that practically no outward commands are necessary. To the unknowing eye, it will look as though the dog is reading your mind. This, of course, is not so, but it looks that way. The dog is reading your attitude, movements, and expression. Remember back in school he learned first by voice, then hand signal, and whistle, but the dog didn't stop learning there. By observation he learns what you are saying. Therefore gradually cut down on the use of signals in the field. This will make your hunt easier and more important, the dog will gain confidence in himself. The trainer who keeps blasting the whistle will sooner or later call his dog while he's on point. This will surely confuse a dog!

Your dog is learning of his own accord to take his cue from you. *You* set the pace for the hunting. One of the biggest errors that new trainers make is to work their dogs through cover too fast. This gives the dog the impression that speed is important, and he may develop a tendency to cover too much ground. Work slowly — the dog will do the same. It will develop thoroughness, and he'll not have a tendency to get out of range.

Teach the dog to go into heavy cover. This is the thorn on the rose. If you want him to go into heavy cover, the way to tell him is to show that you want to hunt too. *You go in.* Command GO IN, give the directional hand signal, and keep repeating the vocal command. Take a deep breath and plunge in yourself. He'll go in too. Soon he'll do it on command alone.

217. You want your dog to go in and hunt, show him that you want to do it too. He'll be in.

WELL, THAT'S IT

I think I have told you enough about your dog and yourself so that you can take over from here. No man could write the answers to all the questions, problems, and situations that will come up. Of course, if he did, he would take all the fun out of training. If anything, now you should know the role of the teacher. But, more important, you know the psychological make-up of the pupil and how to teach him to handle the major situations he will find on the job.

Two last words — good gunning.

Index